The MART

The MART
COMPUTER APPLICATIONS FOR MARKETING

R. N. Maddox
D. A. Schellinck
Dalhousie University

PRENTICE HALL, Englewood Cliffs, New Jersey 07632

Editorial/production supervision: *Maureen Lopez*
Manufacturing Buyers: *Trudy Pisciotti/Bob Anderson*
Acquisitions Editor: *Tim Kent*
Supplement Acquisitions Editor: *Jenny Sheehan*

©1991 by Prentice-Hall, Inc.
A Division of Simon & Schuster
Englewood Cliffs, New Jersey 07632

Printed in the United States of America

10   9   8   7   6   5   4   3   2   1

ISBN 0-13-558842-1   01

Prentice-Hall International (UK) Limited, *London*
Prentice-Hall of Australia Pty. Limited, *Sydney*
Prentice-Hall Canada Inc., *Toronto*
Prentice-Hall Hispanoamericana, S.A., *Mexico*
Prentice-Hall of India Private Limited, *New Delhi*
Prentice-Hall of Japan, Inc., *Tokyo*
Simon & Schuster Asia Pte. Ltd., *Signapore*
Editora Prentice-Hall do Brasil, Ltda., *Rio de Janeiro*

Contents

Acknowledgments

We would like to thank Norm Purdy, Raphael Candela, Jack Webb and Martha Reynolds for their assistance in writing Bob's Bakery, Great Western State Lottery Corporation, Hifax Warranty and Merlin Foods respectively.

We also appreciate the continued support of the Dalhousie School of Business Courseware Development Project which has supplied us with some of the computing power necessary to complete this project. We also wish to thank Mark Maddox for programming assistance.

Finally, we wish to express our appreciation to our wives and families, Heather, Jennifer and Trevor Schellinck and Mary Maddox, who gave up many of the alleged advantages of academic life, including summers, while this project was in progress.

The MART

1 Introduction

What is *The MART?* For that matter, what's marketing? We will attempt to begin answering those questions in the following pages. First, we will introduce you to *The MART,* an innovative approach to the study of marketing. This chapter is very rudimentary, but *essential* if you wish to run these programs with minimum hassle.

Exercises to introduce you to marketing and *The MART's* computer programs follow. These are designed to 1) emphasize the fact that marketing is not just advertising, but a many faceted process and 2) familiarize you with *The MART's* menus and screens. Time spent on these exercises will pay big dividends as you proceed through the book.

1 Introduction to The MART

Welcome to marketing in the last decade of the twentieth century. When you graduate and enter the work place, a microcomputer or a terminal will, undoubtedly, be an integral part of your working life. This text and the accompanying program disks are designed to harness the speed and power of the micro computer to help you, the student, learn about marketing management.

In developing these exercises we adopted one primary rule. That rule was to include an exercise in the package only if the computer facilitated attainment of the learning objectives. For this reason the exercises are biased towards the quantitative, and computational aspects of marketing management. We feel this is as it should be. Using computers for what they do best frees humans for more creative and more intuitive tasks.

This book is not intended to serve as a freestanding course in marketing. You should always read the related chapters in your text before attempting to complete the exercises. We have provided extended coverage of topics only when it was deemed necessary to help the student to understand the inputs to, or the results of an exercise.

Getting Started

Equipment Needed

To run the programs you will need an IBM PC (or true compatible) capable of running MS DOS 2.0 or higher. The programs can be run with a single disk drive, but several run more conveniently with dual drives. (The programs may also be installed in a fixed (hard) drive if you have an extra megabyte of disk space lying around.) Your machine should have an IBM Color Graphics Card (or the equivalent) installed. The visual displays were planned for a color monitor, but are satisfactory in monochrome. Many will not display properly on a color monitor set to monochrome, though we are not sure why you would want to do so.

Necessary
IBM PC or compatible
MS DOS 2.0 or higher
Disk drive
Graphics card
Desirable
2 floppy drives or hard disk
Color Graphics card
Printer

Several programs allow you to save user data or interim results to disk. To do so you will need to have a formatted disk available. If you are not certain how to format a disk, check your computer's operating manual, or ask someone who can help you.

There will be times when you wish to make printed copy of your work using the print screen < Prt Scr > feature of your computer. It should be obvious that you will need a printer to do so. Make sure that the printer is installed and is ready to go before you need it. This is optional. None of the programs require a printer to function properly.

To Begin[1]

Removable Disk

To begin insert a disk with MS DOS (frequently called a BOOT DISK or STARTUP DISK) in the A drive. All disks should be inserted so that the oval cutout enters first and the square notch, or write protect tape is to your left.

---

[1]If *The MART* is installed on a network, check with your instructor or installation manager.

Latch the gate on the drive and turn on your computer and monitor. The drive light will
light up and there will be some whirring as the computer
reads data. When the light goes out remove the DOS disk
and place *The MART's* disk 1 in drive A. Type MART, then
press the Enter (return) key. After some more grumbling
you will see *The MART's* title screen. From this point on
simply follow the prompts.

| Boot machine |
| Insert disk 1 |
| Type "MART" |

Fixed Disk

To install the programs on a fixed disk drive, create a subdirectory to hold them, giving it any
name you choose. Copy all disks into that directory, using copy *.*. Be sure the highest
numbered disk is copied in last. The MAIN.EXE file from this disk must be the one installed
on the hard disk. To run the program change to the new subdirectory and type MART.

Running *The MART*

Watch the displays at the bottom of the screen for instructions. Generally, to move around
in a menu you will use one of the arrow keys on the numeric
keypad to the right hand side of the keyboard. Other keys on
the keypad < End, Home, Pg Up, Pg Dn > are used to
make a selection, begin or end a process or return to the
menu. The instruction, "Press any key," refers to any letter,
< Enter >, the space bar, or the top row of numbers.

| Arrow keys $< \uparrow \leftrightarrow \downarrow >$ |
| move cursor |
| < Pg Dn > makes |
| selection |
| Instructions: |
| bottom line |

In many instances the enter key and < Pg Dn > can be
used interchangeably. If enter is more natural for you, or
your keyboard, give it a try. If you get beeped, you are in one of the programs where we
could not provide this convenience.

We have frequently used the abbreviation for carriage return, C/R, instead of < Enter >,
in on-screen instructions. This is either because it makes more effective use of screen space,
or because the authors are living in the past, when carriage return was the more common
term. The programs assume you will use the keys at the top of the keyboard to type in
numbers. Do not attempt to punctuate numbers with commas, or enter symbols for
dimensions such as $, # or %. Sometimes the computer will insert these after you make an
entry to improve readability.

We have attempted to guard against improper entries such as values that exceed the proper
ranges. The backspace ← key can be used to correct a number before the enter key is pressed.
If you enter an out of range value, you should get "beeped" and see a message reminding you
of the proper values. The message REDO FROM START indicates the computer was

expecting numeric input and you pressed another sort of key. Just type in the proper values.

If you type a wrong value and press <Enter>, just continue. Either you will have a chance to edit the entry later on, or the program runs quickly and you can begin it again, entering the correct values.

If things really get messed up, press <Esc>, which should take you back to a menu. If nothing happens upon pressing <Esc>, you may have inadvertently toggled the <Caps Lock> key. Press <Caps Lock> once and then <Esc>. If that doesn't help, simultaneously press <Ctrl> and <Break>, which should take you back to the DOS prompt. You can then start over.

In many programs there is an element of randomness, just as in the real world. Don't worry if you don't get exactly the same numbers as a fellow student.

2 Seal-Away

Crosby Plastics is considering the introduction of a new line of reusable "freezer to microwave oven" containers tentatively branded as the Seal-Away line. These clear plastic containers can be used to store food in the fridge or freezer and can be used for cooking or reheating food in the microwave oven. Crosby has developed a plastic that can be used to make containers that are clear, allowing the consumer to easily see the contents. But, unlike most existing brands, the plastic cannot be stained by tomato or grape based foods, a frequent consumer complaint. The plastic is also relatively easy to clean compared to the competitors' brands. Food does not stick to the plastic and the plastic does not scratch easily when scrubbed. The new venture team must decide what target market to go after, and whether their new plastic would be part of an optimal marketing strategy.

Crosby is a major manufacturer of plastics, but up to now it has mainly produced containers for the industrial market. Any consumer products it produces are for resale by other companies, who put their own brand on the products. The firm wishes to expand its sales base and feels there is opportunity in the consumer market. The new plastic might give them a competitive advantage, if there is a market for it.

Product Options

Although the company can produce a line of containers with this new high quality plastic, they are considering *two other options* for product quality as well. At the *low end*, Crosby could produce a product that would perform the same function as the existing freezer to microwave containers, but they would be made of a relatively inexpensive plastic which might show stains and could be difficult to clean. The product's major advantage is that it would be inexpensive to produce and would perform the required functions. It was pointed out that many of the consumers did not complain about the staining and cleaning problems and they might prefer the less expensive alternative. On the other hand, studies had shown that some consumers tend to rate a container made with the low quality plastic as more subject to cracking — it isn't.

The *second option* is to produce containers with the same plastic as most existing brands. Crosby's experience in plastics production, and its economies of scale would allow it to price itself near, or below its competitors. The *third option* is to make a premium product with the new non-stain, easy to clean, plastic. While they could have a competitive advantage based on their technological breakthrough, there is doubt whether enough consumers would be willing to pay the higher prices that would have to be charged to cover the higher cost of

6

production. This third product option is fully and economically recyclable, if the containers are physically damaged.

Purchase Situations

Research was conducted to examine the behavior associated with the purchase of microwavable containers. The study found that there were three purchase profiles. First, many people purchase freezer to microwave containers shortly after the purchase of a microwave oven. The purchase is usually made by a spouse or older children buying a birthday or Christmas gift. They visit several department stores before purchasing a set of containers, the children buying sets priced from $10.00 - $20.00, the adults spending $20.00 - $40.00. They tend to compare brands and ask salesclerks for their opinions. These gift giving purchase situations account for 50% of the purchases.

Second, roughly 35% of the purchases are made on impulse at department stores, grocery stores, hardware stores, and even drugstores. These purchases are likely to be made by the main user of the containers. They remember a recent situation where they were short of storage containers and then purchase one or two pieces to fill the gaps.

A third type of purchase situation accounts for the bulk of the remaining purchases (15%). These are purchases in boutiques specializing in kitchen related products. The purchase is made by someone looking for a high quality, fashionable product for their modern kitchen. These people are knowledgeable; many of them read magazines that review these products. Also, they tend to select the store as their first cue for quality and style, and then select a set of containers from among those available at that store. Because they purchase high quality brands their expenditures are considerably higher than average.

Decisions

The firm has several decisions to make. Which type of purchase situation should they target? Then they have to decide on the appropriate product, distribution intensity, advertising level and theme, and production capacity allocated to the brand.

Promotion

Advertising Themes

Three advertising themes were developed by Crosby's advertising agency. These were:

Reduce Spoilage: These advertisements emphasize the value of the containers for storing food, and stress that food is more likely to be reheated and consumed if it is stored in these easy-to-see-through containers that conveniently pop into the microwave. The idea is that the consumer could save money by reducing spoilage.

Added Convenience: These advertisements stress the time-saving advantage of using the product. It is more convenient to store food in these containers as they save time switching from one type of container to another. Using fewer containers reduces clean-up time.

A Beautiful Addition: The product is portrayed as a high tech marvel. It is easy to clean, never staining so that it always looks good, even when used to serve food at the table. These advertisements emphasize the attractiveness of the product, suggesting that it will last a lifetime of use.

Sales Force

Crosby Plastics does not have an existing consumer products sales force. Management has the choice of using wholesale agents, a sales force roughly equivalent to competitors in size, or going with a larger sales force to give themselves a competitive edge.

Production Capacity

Other decisions that will have to be made concern how much to invest in manpower, training and machinery to produce the containers. The company is operating at capacity now and there is an 18 month lead time to purchase and install the machines. Each new machine would be able to produce 300,000 units per year. Not enough production capacity or too much could both lead to losses where there might otherwise be profits.

Manufacturer's Price Options

Price Per Case	. . . .	Low	. . . .	$16.80
		Medium	. . . .	$20.40
		High	. . . .	$30.00

Variable Costs per Case

Production cost	. . . .	Low Quality	. . . . . .	$9.00
		Standard Quality	. . . .	$10.93
		Premium Quality	. . .	$12.86
Distribution Cost	. . .	Exclusive Distribution		$2.75
		Selective	. . . .	$3.00
		Intensive	. . . .	$3.70

Fixed Costs
($000)

Advertising Costs . . .	Minimum Expenditure . .	$200,000
	Meet Competition	$600,000
	High Expenditure	$1,400,000
Sales Promotion . . .	Minimum Expenditure . .	$100,000
Costs	Meet Competition	$300,000
	High Expenditure	$500,000
Sales force costs . . .	Wholesale Agents	$200,000
	Standard Sales force	$400,000
	Extra Sales force	$550,000
Overhead	One Machine	$150,000
	Two Machines	$250,000
	Three Machines	$325,000

Strategic Choices

Several members of the new venture team have different opinions about what is likely to be the best strategy. Mary MacIntosh, production manager feels that targeting the gift giving market with either the standard or the low quality product is the best alternative. She pointed out that this is by far the largest market, and the company's objective is to expand sales. Given their cost advantages, she feels they will be able to capture a large part of this market, leading to even greater economies of scale, and higher profits.

It was Joseph Skowron from R&D who suggested that a price of $30 be considered, even though this is far above the cost of production. Despite arguments that this will severely limit sales, ("We'll hardly be able to sell enough to keep one machine busy!"), he insists that a high price might require less advertising, sales promotion and production equipment to generate a profit. This will reduce overall risk and investment.

Ray Kehoe, the sales manager, supports the option of going after the impulse market. He feels that consumers are considerably less price sensitive under those circumstances. "All we have to do is make sure our brand is there, and make sure they notice it, when they make the decision to buy."

Nothing was resolved however, so they called you in as a marketing consultant, to suggest an appropriate strategy for their new Seal–Away line.

The Strategy Program

The Marketing Strategy Model program allows you to select the alternatives available in the Seal–Away case and to see how profitable your selected strategy would be. The result of your selections is given to you in the form of an income statement, so that you can judge the relative impact of the various elements of the marketing mix on profits. While you can optimize profits through repeated trial and error, we hope that you will apply what you have learned from your text to devise a more systematic search for a solution.

Use the up and down arrows to select strategy elements and the left and right arrows to select appropriate options for that element. When you have a target market and an appropriate marketing mix selected, hit <Pg Dn> to see the result of your selections. Hit <Pg Up> to go back and change the strategy elements. Once you have decided on a strategy for a particular target market use the print screen <Prt Sc> key to print your decisions and results.

One purpose of this program is to emphasis that a good fit between the target market and the marketing mix is an essential part of target marketing. Therefore, the sales listed are for that target market only. Thus, while for one target market a lower price may lead to higher sales, it may have the opposite effect on sales to another target market. The sales figure will only reflect the response of the selected target market.

Section_____   Name_____

Student Number_____

Assignment

1.   Fill in the table below with your strategic selections and the resulting income figures.

Strategy Element Selections

	Gift Giving	Impulse	Modern Kitchen
Product Quality	_____	_____	_____
Market Exposure	_____	_____	_____
Promotional Efforts			
Advertising level	_____	_____	_____
Advertising copy	_____	_____	_____
Sales Promotion	_____	_____	_____
Sales force support	_____	_____	_____
Price level	_____	_____	_____
Plant investment	_____	_____	_____

Income Statements

	Gift Giving	Impulse	Modern Kitchen
Revenue			
Unit sales	_____	_____	_____
Average price	_____	_____	_____
Total revenue	_____	_____	_____
Less variable costs			
Production	_____	_____	_____
Distribution	_____	_____	_____
Contribution to overhead	_____	_____	_____

SEAL–AWAY

Less fixed costs
    Advertising   _____   _____   _____
    Sales promotion   _____   _____   _____
    Sales force costs   _____   _____   _____
    Factory & overhead   _____   _____   _____

    Net income   _____   _____   _____

2.   What elements of Mary MacIntosh's arguments are right, which are wrong?

_____

_____

_____

_____

3.   What elements of Joseph Skowron's arguments are right, which are wrong?

_____

_____

_____

_____

4.   Which elements of Ray Kehoe's arguments are right, which are wrong?

_____

_____

_____

_____

5. If you had to go after one target market initially, which would you go after and why?

_____

_____

_____

_____

6. How would you classify each of the consumer goods purchased by each of the target markets?

Consumer Goods Classification

Gift Giving _____

Impulse _____

Modern Kitchen _____

7. What direction do these classifications give you in selecting the appropriate marketing mix?

_____

_____

_____

_____

II The Spreadsheet Model

The MART includes a spreadsheet which is suited to solving a particular type of problem. Its functions are intentionally limited to preclude the necessity of learning a complex set of commands just to accomplish a few simple, but computationally burdensome tasks.

The model is dedicated to problems, such as new product checklists or attitude models, in which a set of alternatives, such as products, are rated on a number of attributes or dimensions and the attributes, are, in turn, rated as to importance. An alternative's total score, S_o, is the sum, over all attributes, of the alternative's rating on a dimension, r_{io}, multiplied by the importance, w_i of that dimension. (Technically, these are called weighted, linear, compensatory models.)

$$S_o = \Sigma_{(i=1)}^{n} \; w_i * r_{io}$$

Assume the situation portrayed in the matrix in Table 1. A manufacturer is seeking to narrow its list of suppliers for a component part from three to two. The only attributes

Table 1 Spreadsheet Illustration

	Importance	Average Days		
		Excello Inc.	SpeedE	LazAlong
Order time	5	6	5	7
Fill-in order Time	3	3	4	3
Total Score		39	37	44

being considered are average order time and time for filling emergency orders. The manufacturer considers the importance of average order time to be three on a ten point scale and time for fill-in orders to be five. (One is best.) From its records it has found the average number of days for each kind of order shown in the table. The manufacturer would drop LazAlong from its list of suppliers based upon its score (44 = 5 X 7 + 3 X 3).

In the preceding example the alternatives were rated using a natural and common unit of measure, days. In other instances, such a common denominator is not present. For example, the dimensions might have been average order time and *willingness to respond* to fill-in orders. Such cases can be handled by assigning each alternative a rating on each dimension using, say, a 10 point scale and then using these ratings just as we used days.

The direction of the importance and rating scales (whether high or low values are favorable) is immaterial as long as they are consistent. If higher ratings are more favorable then higher values must indicate greater importance.

In the example the calculations were performed using the raw weights. It is frequently advantageous to normalize these values, i.e., convert them to decimal fractions totalling 1.0. In the example these weights would be 0.625 (5/8) and 0.375 (3/8). This approach is the one used by Spreadsheet.

Entering Data

The Spreadsheet Model can handle problems with up to six alternatives and as many as nine attributes or dimensions. After specifying the number of each, you will be presented with an appropriately dimensioned matrix display. You will then have the opportunity to enter the names of each alternative and attribute. You can skip over any or all of the names, leaving them blank. It is worth the little bit of time it takes to make the entries in case you later wish to use < Shift – Prt Sc > to make a printed copy of your work.

After names are entered you can enter the importance and attribute ratings, in any order. Use the cursor keys to move from cell to cell. Normalized importance weights will be computed and displayed as soon as all weights are entered. After the normalized weights appear, Spreadsheet will calculate a solution after each rating is entered. (If you find this annoying enter the alternative ratings first.)

Changing Entries

Any value may be changed at any time. To change an alternative's rating, simply move to the desired cell and enter the new value. A new solution will automatically be calculated, if a full set of importance weights has been entered.

Changing *importance weights* is done in one of three ways. If a full set of weights has *not* been entered just move to the correct cell and type the new number.

If all weights have been entered, you may make the change to either the normalized or raw weights, as indicated by a prompt at the bottom of the screen. Press <Pg Dn> to initiate the change mode. If you wish to change the *normalized* weights, simply enter a new decimal fraction. The program will consider that value fixed and make proportional adjustments to the remaining weights so that the sum remains 1.0. (If your weights were 0.25, 0.25, 0.50 and you changed the larger value to .60, the new weights would be 0.20, 0.20, 0.60.)

To make changes to the *raw* weights press <Home> after going into the change mode. The original (raw) weights will be displayed for all cells, except the one you have indicated you want to change. Enter the new value and a new set of normalized weights will be displayed along with a fresh solution.

III Target Market Analysis

3 Consumer Behavior: Attitudes

Attitudes are an important variable in understanding consumer behavior. Attitudes are important because we believe they are related to behavior, whether that behavior be voting for a political candidate, choosing a mate for life, or selecting a brand of toothpaste. Research findings on the attitude behavior relationship are mixed, and indicate attitudes, as researchers define and measure them, are but one of a large and complex set of factors giving rise to our choices.

Researchers have proposed a number of models to explain how attitudes are formed. One of the most understandable, and one of the most popular among practicing managers and researchers is shown below.[1] The model simply says that the attitude towards some object,

$$A_o = \Sigma_{(i=1)}^n w_i * b_{io}$$

A_o, can be explained using n attributes, or evaluative criteria. The importance of each evaluative criterion, w_i, is multiplied by the belief about the standing of object o on that dimension, b_{io} (the rating of the object).

This all seems very complicated, but it really isn't. All it says is that our overall attitude towards something results from beliefs about it on a number of dimensions used in evaluating that category of objects. Our attitudes towards a supermarket might result from our appraisals of its price level, merchandise selection, meat and produce quality, and the friendliness of its personnel. In forming an overall attitude, which is sort of a summary statement, we give greater weight to dimensions that we feel are more important. If we feel friendly personnel is twice as important as a wide assortment of groceries, it would have twice the influence in the formation of our attitude.

The model shown above is merely a way of expressing these ideas in more rigorous terms. No one claims we consciously go through the process of multiplying and summing terms. The equation is merely a way of describing an, ultimately, unknowable process.

---

[1]A different and more complex formulation will be introduced in the discussion of product positioning. See p. 153.

4 Cozy Hearth Stove

Cozy Hearth Stove store was founded as Country Fireplace Accessories in 1964. In the seventies repeated oil shortages and the soaring prices of fossil fuels resulted in growing interest in wood stoves as an alternate, or supplemental source of heat. Country Fireplace had shifted its merchandise mix to emphasize stoves and related items in order to capitalize on this trend. The firm had changed its name in 1978, to better reflect its offering. Stove sales were about equally divided between the do-it-yourself market and building and renovation contractors.

Carter Gates, the owner manager, had traditionally relied entirely on his gut feel in selecting suppliers and buying new merchandise. He simply bought what he thought looked good. If he was proven to be correct, he continued to order the item. If an item didn't sell, he marked it down, moved it out, and tried to do better next time.

A recent presentation by a marketing executive at the Better Business Bureau had convinced Gates that a more consumer oriented approach might better serve both his customers' interest and his own self interest. He had decided to factor a little informal research into the buying process.

Four stoves were under consideration for addition to his line for the coming season. One would be selected. Gates recruited members of his bridge club, whom he considered to be "average folks," to rate the candidates. While refreshments were being served, he passed around descriptive brochures and had one member of each couple complete a rating form. Respondents first rated a set of attributes as to importance, using a seven point scale where seven was very important. Next, they rated each of the candidates, on each attribute, on ten point scales. High scores indicated more desirable ratings. Average ratings are shown in Table 2.

Table 2 Ratings of Stoves under Consideration

Attributes	Importance	Stove Ratings			
		Thor	Titan	Vulcan	Cheery Hearth
BTU Output	7	1	10	10	7
Safety	5	3	2	5	3
Ease of Installation	3	7	6	5	10
Appearance	4	1	3	5	10
Small Size	6	10	8	4	2
Cooking Surface	5	1	2	8	7
Low Price	4	6	5	4	5
Fuel Efficiency	6	1	7	6	4

Assignment

Select the Spreadsheet model from *The MART's* menu and answer the following questions.

1.   Which stove should be ordered based on the ratings given?

_____

2.   Would your decision change if the importance of appearance had been 7.0, instead of 4.0?

_____

3.   Which should Carter choose if all attributes were equally important?

_____

4.   Which would be chosen if price were the only criterion to be considered?

_____

5.   What factors other than consumer attitudes should be factored into Carter's decision?

_____

6.   What faults can you find with Carter's research?

_____

_____

_____

_____

5 Gudrun's Fine Foods

Rockies Reworks was a management consulting firm concentrating on the restaurant trade. Its specialty was in developing strategic plans for turning around marginal and failing restaurants. Most of their projects were for restaurants about to be sold by owners approaching retirement or the executors of the estates of restaurants whose owners had retired, permanently. Rockies' newest client, Gudrun's Fine Food, was an exception. Gudrun, a vigorous woman of early middle-age, was very much alive and wanted very much to stay in the business.

Gudrun Ericksen had taken over a mom and pop restaurant in a medium sized northern grain belt city in 1984. She brought in a whole new offering. It specialized in hearty meals featuring generous servings of plain, but very well prepared food. The noon Thresher's Special, a heavy meat and potatoes sort of a lunch, had proven particularly popular with local businessmen. The decor had been described as "early Bavarian farmhouse."

Business had gone very well for awhile, but had been off sharply for about 18 months. Gudrun's accountant had recommended that she contact Rockies Reworks based upon the favorable experience of another of his clients.

Ralph Kirkland was the senior partner handling the Gudrun's Fine Foods account. His initial impression was that Gudrun's offering was an excellent response to a time that had passed. The health and fitness craze had come to Northland a little late, but it had arrived about the same time as Gudrun's. Rather than make recommendations based on his hunch, Kirkland had commissioned a study of attitudes towards Gudrun's and its two major competitors.

In the study respondents rated a set of attributes describing a restaurant as to their importance by dividing a fixed sum (100 points) among the attributes. The attribute set had been developed in Rockies Reworks' studies over the years and modified to fit the immediate problem. Respondents were instructed to allocate the points so that if one attribute was twice as important as another, it got twice as many points. They then rated the three restaurants on each attribute, using seven point scales, with seven being the best rating possible. Some results of the study are shown in Table 3.

Table 3 Gudrun's Fine Foods Study

Attribute	Importance	Restaurant Ratings		
		Gudrun's	Chez Maison	Neptune's Larder
Home Style Food	3	10	1	1
Hearty Servings	5	9	1	3
Sophisticated Setting	14	2	10	5
Cuisine for the Eighties	24	1	7	7
Features Seafood Selection	18	2	5	7
Low Cholesterol Menu	21	1	4	5
Simple Decor	6	6	2	1
Friendly, Homey Feeling	2	5	3	3
Low Prices	7	4	2	3

Section_____   Name_____

                          Student Number_____

Assignment

Select the Spreadsheet model from *The MART's* menu and answer the following questions.

1.   Which restaurant should be most popular based on the attitude survey?

      _____

2.   Would this change if the importance ratings of Hearty Servings and Low Cholesterol Menu were reversed?

      _____

3.   Which should be most popular if all attributes were equally important?

      _____

4.   Which would be chosen if price were the only criterion to be considered?

      _____

5.   Assume Kirkland recommended that Gudrun's attempt to change customer attitudes. What general strategies are suggested by the attitude model?

      _____

6.   What aspects of the offering would you recommend that Gudrun consider changing?

      _____

7.   Do the changes you recommended constitute a refinement of the offering, or an entirely new strategy?

      _____

8. The attitude study interviewed a random sample of the adult population. Is there information you would like other than the summary table shown above?

_____

_____

_____

_____

6 Market Segmentation

You should thoroughly understand your text's discussion of market segmentation and target marketing before attempting these exercises. We will review only the criteria for judging the usefulness of a target market since these are necessary to use the market segmentation program successfully.

The very notion of market segmentation requires that the chosen segment responds differently to some marketing activity than the mass market. Though it is easiest to think of a segment being differentially attracted to a product that uniquely meets its needs, this behavioral difference can be with respect to any element of the marketing mix.

Given that a group of customers has been identified that promises to exhibit the required behavioral difference, three factors must be considered before choosing to target this segment: measurability, accessibility and substantiality.

Measurability (identifiability). We must be able to measure the size and purchasing power of a target market. Some potential segmenting variables are difficult to measure. Taking an extreme case, it would be of little value to know our product was particularly attractive to those who had recently committed a traffic offense without getting caught.

Accessibility (reachability). The individuals constituting a segment must be accessible so that they can be presented with our offering. It does no good to know that some group would respond well to an advertising appeal, if group members' exposure habits do not allow us to reach them with the message.

Measurability and accessibility are a particular problem when we try to use softer, more behavioral dimensions to segment a market. Say our product appeals to those for whom low price is an important attribute. We cannot list or differentially reach a segment defined only on this piece of information. We must usually attempt to discover the demographic characteristics of those valuing this attribute. We then direct our marketing efforts to those demographic groups.

Substantiality (sizability). A market segment must be large enough to be served at a profit. This can be a problem when the cost of developing and presenting the marketing mix is high, when the total market is small, or when multiple variables are used to define a segment.

The Segmentation Program

This program will allow you to solve cases requiring the selection of target markets using consumer research data. Only a subset of the questions from a larger questionnaire have been included in order to keep your task (and the time required) manageable. These questions are your potential segmenting variables.

Defining A Segment

When the program begins you will first have the opportunity to designate a case to analyze. After the program reads the case data, you will be able to select a variable which will be used to identify a target market. You do this by entering the variable's number at the prompt. For example, if you believe the consumption of your product will vary by income level, you would enter the question number for income.

If you have not read the discussion of segmentation, you should do so now. To be of value a segment must usually be identified on a variable which allows us to identify those belonging to the segment. Conceptually, we may define our market segment using behavioral variables, such as attitudes or preferences. If we are to reach that segment, we must determine the demographic characteristics of that group and then target customers with those characteristics. Ultimately, a segment must, usually, be defined in terms of hard, demographic descriptors.

After a segmenting variable is designated you will be asked to specify the level(s) — responses — on that variable which identify individuals who will be included in the segment you are defining. If you believe persons with larger incomes are more promising targets, you would choose the codes for the higher income categories. Use the cursor keys to move from one response code to another. <Pg Dn> will indicate to the program that a particular code is to be included. Pressing <Pg Dn> a second time will remove the code from the segment description. Press <End> when you are done with a variable.

You may choose as many as four segmenting variables. If you wish to use fewer than four, as will probably be the case, simply press <Enter> when the program asks for the next variable number.

After a segment is chosen, the program will sort the cases to determine those that are in the segment you have identified and those that are not. When this has been accomplished, a graphic display will show the proportion of the sample that are in (white) and that are not in (magenta) your segment. This screen will also show the variables, and levels thereon, used in defining the segment.

You will then be asked to identify the dependent or criterion variable, by number. This is a measure of the behavior in which you are interested, such as purchases, purchase intentions or preference.

Graphic Display

After the program completes its computations, a second screen will appear. The top portion will be unchanged. At the bottom right you will see the means and medians on the criterion variable for the total sample (green) and those in and not in your target market. Bar graphs comparing the means will be printed.

It is useful to examine the distribution of responses as well as the measures of central tendency (mean and median). The bottom left quadrant shows the proportion of the total sample, and of those in and not in your segment, selecting each of the responses on the criterion variable.

Be sure to consider the top and bottom information in tandem. A display indicating that 50% of your segment are certain to buy a product, may only indicate that one of the two people in the segment you defined gave that response. The top of the screen will help you determine substantiality: whether a segment is large enough to warrant targeting. The bottom indicates whether **your** segment really differs from the rest of the population.

After you finish viewing the results screen, you will be offered three options. First, you may choose to retain the segment you defined and select another criterion variable. Second, you may redefine your target market segment. Finally, you may return to the market segmentation menu.

7 Schmidt's Packers

Donald Kay was president of Schmidt's Packers, which operated meat packing plants in a number of midwestern cities. As he approached retirement, he reflected, with increasing frequency, on changes affecting his industry. He didn't feel all had been for the better. Some, such as regulations improving plant sanitation, were, obviously, in the consumer's best interest. On the other hand, he didn't feel that printing "tongue" or "stomach" on a bologna ingredient list, instead of "meat byproducts" was much of an advance.

Processed meats, particularly frankfurters, were Kay's pet peeve. He didn't believe that the progression from the bad old days of an unspecified mixture of meat products and grains, to "all meat," to "all beef," to chicken dogs and turkey dogs, had been progress, at all. The reduction in spicing and flavorings so as not to offend the mass palate had resulted in what he felt was a pallid imitation of the real thing. He longed for the luncheon meats and frankfurters that had disappeared in the fifties.

Project Schultz

Unlike many in a similar situation, Mr. Kay did more than reminisce. The company's product development labs in Cincinnati were charged with the task of taking a leap back in time. Project Schultz, named after the bumbling German sergeant on "Hogan's Heros," was to resurrect Schmidt's original recipes, adapt them to currently available ingredients and manufacturing techniques, and develop a product line that matched Kay's memories.

Wilhelm Robb, the director of project Schultz, recognized that he faced a two pronged challenge: marketing and manufacturing. The turn to poultry based products reflected not only raw materials costs, but also consumer concerns about dietary cholesterol. He didn't believe the added costs of red meat based products was much of a problem, since the line was to be promoted as a specialty product and should be able to carry a premium price. Cholesterol worries were a bigger problem, because the upscale market to which the product would be targeted showed the greatest concern.

The lab and production engineering had come through. They had developed a manufacturing process for extracting 99.9% of the fats from meat. The cholesterol-free residue was then mixed with hydrogenated corn oil which provided the fat necessary to proper mouth feel in some of the items. When used in the old recipes these mixtures were indistinguishable from the natural product. Best of all, the extraction process left no residue that would have to be shown on an ingredient list. Robb found it amusing that one of mankind's oldest processed food products, sausage, would be produced by a very high tech process.

Robb's initial mandate was to develop products conforming to Kay's specifications. This had been accomplished. According to company policy, Project Schultz would now be augmented with representatives from marketing, to take the product to the consumer.

At their first meeting Martin Osler, the marketing VP, had asked "Who, other than Donald Kay, wants this stuff?" Robb's decisive "Well, uh ... " hadn't really seemed to be an adequate answer. Osler went on to suggest that those who shared Kay's memories grew fewer in number with each passing year and those remaining might not offer a very attractive marketing opportunity.

Product Tests

Nevertheless, Osler needed Kay's blessing if he was to succeed Kay as President. He assigned one of his star researchers to Project Schultz to see what could be done to salvage a bad situation. Brian Robertson had been responsible for the marketing research on several successful product introductions. Since product development was complete, he recommended in-home product tests, beginning with frankfurters.

Interviewers called upon a random sample of homes, gave each a package of the product, and asked them to serve them prior to the expiry date printed thereon. They were told that this was a new product, but not how it was supposed to differ from products already on the market.

The package looked as if a brand name had been obliterated. In fact, none had been chosen. An ingredients list, completely conforming to legal requirements, was printed on the side. "Cholesterol Free" was featured prominently on both the front and the back of each package.

The interviewers contacted participating households by telephone two days prior to the expiry date on the package they had been given. The purpose of this call was ostensibly to arrange a time to deliver the gift they had been promised as a reward for participating. The timing of the phone call was chosen to remind those who had not tried the franks to do so.

When the gift was delivered, the interviewer obtained product ratings and other information. They interviewed an adult randomly selected from among those identified as doing at least some of the household's grocery shopping. Several questions from the questionnaire are shown below. (The variable numbers in *The Mart's* data set are the same as the question numbers.)

Project Schultz Questionnaire
Selected Questions

1. When were you born?

   1. After 1967
   2. 1958 - 1967
   3. 1948 - 1957
   4. 1938 - 1947
   5. before 1938

2. What bracket would include your household income, after taxes last year?

   1. less than $10,000
   2. $10,001 - $20,000
   3. $20,001 - $30,000
   4. $30,001 - $40,000
   5. over $40,000

3. How many persons over the age of three are there in your household?

   1. One
   2. Two
   3. Three
   4. Four
   5. Five or more

4. How frequently do you serve processed meats such as frankfurters and luncheon meats?

   1. Never
   2. Less than once a month
   3. One or two times a month
   4. Once a week
   5. More than once a week

Please rate the product you tested on the following factors.

		Poor	Average			Excellent
5.	Flavor	1	2	3	4	5
6.	Texture	1	2	3	4	5
7.	Nutritional Value	1	2	3	4	5

8. If this brand of frankfurters were available in your supermarket, how likely would you be to purchase it?

   1. No chance, almost no chance (1 chance in 100)
   2. Some probability (3 in 10)
   3. Fairly good possibility (5 in 10)
   4. Probable (7 in 10)
   5. Almost certain (99 chances in 100)

Section_____   Name_____

                          Student Number_____

Assignment

Use *The MART* to help answer the following questions. Select Market Segmentation then Schmidt's Packers from *The MART's* menus.

1.   How do respondents, as a whole, rate the product on

        a. flavor? (*Hint:* To obtain the mean and frequency distribution for "flavor," select any category on one of the first three variables as your segmenting variable and variable five as your criterion variable.)

        _____

        b. texture?

        _____

        c. nutritional value?

        _____

2.   How likely did the average respondent say he or she was to buy the product, if it became available?

        _____

3.   Does any subset of the respondents seem more likely to buy the product than the rest?

        _____

        If so, what level(s) on what variable(s) identify this segment?

        _____

        What portion of the respondents are in this segment?

        _____

4.   What is the average score on variable eight for

the target segment identified above?

_____

the remainder of the sample?

_____

5.   The mean, or any other measure of central tendency can often be misleading. What proportion (you'll have to estimate from the frequency distributions) indicated that they would "probably" or "almost certainly" buy the product for

your target segment?

_____

the remainder of the sample?

_____

6.   How do the mean ratings of product attributes by your target segment compare to those of respondents not in your segment?

	In Selected Segment	Not in Selected Segment
Flavor	_____	_____
Texture	_____	_____
Nutritional Value	_____	_____

8 CompCom, Inc.

Mindy Picard was sort of a Stephen Jobs in a skirt, without his technical expertise. In the mid seventies she had become interested in electronics and had assembled several of the rudimentary computer kits that were on the market at the time. One had worked well enough to be of use in her business.

Mindy considered herself to be a merchant, pure and simple. In addition to a fabric store she had inherited from her mother, she was a partner in, or had invested in, ten other retail businesses ranging from a fast food franchise to a building supply store.

In 1979 she saw her first Apple home computer and fell in love with the machine and the concept. Within a few days she sold off enough of her other interests to raise the cash to open Computer Solutions, Burlington's first home computer store. She had to do it on her own as her former partners and her banker looked on home computers as "Faddish toys for those who had nothing better upon which to waste their money."

Mindy's store succeeded where many founded at the same time failed. Feminist journalists sought her out and featured her in articles proclaiming the superiority of the female as an entrepreneur. Mindy agreed to the interviews and accepted the accolades because the publicity was good for business.

Ms Picard had her own explanation for her success which had nothing to do with sexist rhetoric. She had come to computer retailing as a seasoned merchant, and viewed computers, peripherals and programs as stock to be managed. Many of her failed competitors were technical junkies who became enamored of a piece of hardware and decided they could make a killing by letting the public buy it. Her staff were promoting applications and, as the name indicated, solutions to problems while others were trying to sell bits, bytes and chips.

CompCom: Resolving A Split Personality

CompCom — short for computers and communications — had been spun off as a separate entity in 1985. A growing portion of her sales had been to businesses and professionals. It had become increasingly difficult to serve home and business users with the same staff. CompCom was dedicated to serving commercial customers.

Mindy had a good track record for identifying emerging trends and products that were destined to succeed. She had been among the first to stock the IBM PC. She had taken on

Compaq so early that people thought the signs in her windows were a misspelling of something. She was the first retailer in the area to handle laser printers.

Fax

Despite her many successes, Ms Picard now realized that she had missed a big one. She had believed the facsimile (fax) market would be small and that the need for document transmission would be met by a limited number of machines, operated at central locations, by the Post Office and the commercial courier services. Mindy was determined, but not pigheaded. She was willing to admit that she had been wrong about fax and that she should have the machines in stock.

Customer Survey

Not having "grown up" with the fax market, Mindy was not sure who the customers would be or what features they might be looking for in a machine. She had hired a marketing researcher specializing in executive interviews to survey a sample of her CompCom customers to get a feel for the fax market.

Personal interviews were conducted with the individual in each organization responsible for purchasing computer or communications equipment. Appointments for the interviews had been arranged over the telephone. Completed questionnaires were obtained from over 90% of those drawn for the sample. The high response rate was attributed to the subject's being of interest to respondents, and to the persistence and flexibility, "any time, day or night," of the interviewers.

Selected questions from the interview guide are shown below. Responses were recorded by the interviewers. The variable numbers in the CompCom data set are the same as the question numbers.

CompCom Questionnaire
Selected Questions

1. Type of business or organization.

    1. Manufacturing
    2. Financial/Commercial
    3. Retail/Wholesale
    4. Professional (MD's, Accountants, Lawyers, etc.)
    5. Government/Nonprofit

2. Number of employees in Burlington metropolitan area.

    1.   1 - 5
    2.   6 - 10
    3. 11 - 15
    4. 16 - 30
    5.   > 30

3. Number of letters and documents sent per week by express mail and commercial courier services.

    1. Fewer than one
    2.   1 - 2
    3.   3 - 5
    4.   6 - 10
    5.   > 10

How important would the following be to you in selecting a fax machine? (Interviewers were trained to explain these in detail.)

	Not at all Important				Extremely Important
4. Delayed transmission to take advantage of cheaper phone rates.	1	2	3	4	5
5. Memory capacity of ten pages or more.	1	2	3	4	5
6. Provisions for confidentiality/ security	1	2	3	4	5
7. Rapid Transmission speed	1	2	3	4	5

8. How likely are you to purchase a fax machine from a Burlington supplier in the next six months?

	Not at all Likely				Very Likely
	1	2	3	4	5

Assignment

Use *The MART* to help answer the following questions. Select Market Segmentation then CompCom from *The MART's* menus.

1.   How do respondents, as a whole, rate the importance of

a. delayed transmission?   (*Hint:* To obtain the mean and frequency distribution for delayed transmission, select any category on one of the first three variables as your segmenting variable and variable four as your criterion variable.)

_____

b. memory capacity?

_____

c. confidentiality?

_____

d. transmission speed?

_____

2.   How likely did the respondents, on average, say they were to buy a fax from a local supplier in the next six months?

_____

3.   Does any subset of the respondents seem more likely to buy the product than the rest?

_____

If so, what level(s) on what variable(s) identify this segment?

_____

     CompCom, Inc.

What portion of the respondents are in this segment?

_____

4. What is the average score on variable eight for

the target segment identified above?

_____

the remainder of the sample?

_____

5. The mean, or any other measure of central tendency can often be misleading. What proportion (you'll have to estimate from the frequency distributions) indicated that they would probably or almost certainly buy the product for

your target segment?

_____

the remainder of the sample?

_____

6. How do the mean ratings of product attributes by your target segment compare to those of respondents not in your segment?

	In Selected Segment	Not in Selected Segment
delayed transmission	_____	_____
memory capacity	_____	_____
confidentiality	_____	_____
transmission speed	_____	_____

9 Marketing to Organizations

Marketing to organizations differs in many ways from the marketing of consumer goods. The objective of this model is to allow you to explore and examine the impact of one of these differences: the nature of the demand curves facing those selling goods to intermediate customers.

Select Organizational Marketing from *The MART's* menu. You will first be presented with a choice of cases. Next, you must choose whether to examine demand at the industry or company level.

Industry Analysis. If you choose Industry Analysis, you will be given a recent industry price and indicators of market potential. You will then be asked to specify a new *industry* price. The model will determine the quantity all suppliers can expect to sell at this new price and the industry's total revenue. After at least two trial prices have been entered, you may opt to see a graph of the demand curve after any price is entered.

Company Analysis. If Company Analysis is chosen, you will be given an estimate of prevailing prices and indicators of market potential. You will then be asked to specify a new *company* price. The model will estimate competitors' and customers' responses and determine the results for the industry as a whole and for the company. Graphs of the resulting demand curve can be called after at least two trial prices have been entered.

10 Consolidated Grundel Grips

CGG, Inc., formerly Consolidated Grundel Grips, is one of three suppliers of Grundel Grips (GGs) to the North American automakers. Every new car manufactured requires three pairs of GGs to protect its wiring harnesses. Off-shore manufacturers use a different type of part, costing around $3.00 per auto, to accomplish the same purpose. GGs last the life of an automobile, so there is essentially no aftermarket. GGs account for about 20% of CGG's sales and 40% of profits.

GGs are made to specifications adopted throughout the industry and any single supplier could satisfy at least 50% of industry demand using existing capacity. Pricing is, therefore, viewed as extremely important by CGG and, presumably, by its competitors. Prices last year averaged $0.20 per GG or $1.20 per automobile. CGG's direct (variable) manufacturing costs are close to 50% of last year's selling price. Selling, overhead and administrative expenses of $600,000 are expected to be allocated to the product in the coming year.

Market shares tend to be stable. The auto manufacturers prefer using multiple suppliers to protect themselves against interruptions in the flow of parts which could shut down an entire auto plant. As long as the price is right, any GG manufacturer can pretty much count on receiving its historic share of an automaker's orders. The auto manufacturers are concerned about the reduction in the number of GG suppliers in recent years. Even if a price is high, a GG maker can count on getting a dribble of orders, as long as it is not too far out of line, just to keep the number of suppliers from declining further.

You have been hired by CGG's marketing department and assigned the task of analyzing its pricing problems. Interviews with marketing and production executives have revealed several factors bearing on your task. First, direct manufacturing costs are truly variable over any foreseeable range of output. Second, the part used by the offshore manufacturers requires less labor to install and would be preferred to GGs, if GGs cost more than $2.75 per automobile. Third, CGG senior management would not agree to price below direct manufacturing costs for any period of time. Fourth, at lower prices GGs find some applications in trucks, construction equipment and farm machinery. Finally, your pricing objective is to attempt to maximize profit.

Section_____   Name_____

                                                   Student Number_____

Assignment

A.   Before approaching the computer, answer the following questions.

1.   In what type of market environment (pure competition, monopoly, etc.) does CGG
     compete? Explain your reasoning.

     _____

        _____   ┌─────────────────────────────┐
                                                   │ . . . . │
        _____   │ . . . . │
                                                   │ . . . . │
        _____   │ . . . . │
                                                   │ . . . . │
                                                   │ . . . . │
                                                   │ . . . . │
2.   What should the industry demand curve look   │ . . . . │
     like? (Draw it in the block on the right.)   │ . . . . │
                                                   │ . . . . │
                                                   │ . . . . │
        _____   │ . . . . │
                                                   └─────────────────────────────┘
        _____

     _____

3.   How should CGG's sales respond to changes in its price?

     _____

B. Select Marketing to Organizations from *The MART's* menu and complete the following exercises.

1. Run the *industry analysis*, trying various prices covering the relevant range. Try enough prices to get a solid feeling for the shape of the demand curve. Record the results below.

Price	Industry Quantity (millions)	Industry Total Revenue (millions)
0.60	_____	_____
_____	_____	_____
_____	_____	_____
_____	_____	_____
0.20	_____	_____
_____	_____	_____
_____	_____	_____
0.10	_____	_____

2. Run the *company analysis*. Try several prices below and above the "recent price". Complete the following table.

Prevailing price indicated was _____

CGG's Price	Industry Price	CGG's			
		Market Share	Unit Sales (millions)	Sales($) (millions)	Contribution($) (millions)
0.60	____	_____	_____	_____	_____
____	____	_____	_____	_____	_____
____	____	_____	_____	_____	_____
____	____	_____	_____	_____	_____
0.20	____	_____	_____	_____	_____
____	____	_____	_____	_____	_____
____	____	_____	_____	_____	_____
0.10	____	_____	_____	_____	_____

3. Plot the demand curves for all GG manufacturers (industry demand curve) and for CGG on a piece of graph paper, or in the block below.

Allowing for random fluctuations built into the model, does this bear out your expectations recorded above (A.2 and A.3)?

_____

_____

4. Both curves show a sharp bend or inflection. Are these caused by the same factor(s)?

_____

_____

_____

_____

_____

11 Jeff's Jumpers

Robert Lavigne was founder and owner of Jeff's Jumpers. The jumpers were small hardware devices used to quickly connect lighting fixtures to the wiring of a house when the fixtures were being installed. They could be used with any sort of a light, but found their greatest application in ceiling lights which took longer and required overhead work, which many installers found uncomfortable. Building codes permitted, but did not mandate use of the product.

The name Jeff's Jumpers was chosen simply because Robert, who had a taste for alliteration, thought it was catchy. He had begun the process of registering it as a trademark a couple of years ago. However, "jumpers" was pretty much accepted as the generic name for the product, so he had not followed through.

Jumpers were sold primarily through electrical supply houses to general and electrical contractors for installation in new construction. Jeff's and two competitors each had about a one-third market share. Because of quantity discounts a given wholesaler would only stock one brand at a time. However, loyalty was nonexistent. A purchasing agent would switch suppliers for a penny a pair.

The jumper was definitely a low tech, labor intensive product. Any of the three firms could double its output in the time it took to hire additional, minimally skilled, workers for the production line.

Each fixture in which they were used took one pair of Jumpers. Competition was from plain old wire nuts which served the same purpose. Jumpers saved time, but were not economically competitive at prices above $1.00 a unit, which translated into a manufacturer's price of $.50 a pair. Some demand might exist above that point if contractors humored their installers who preferred using jumpers. At low prices hardware retailers and lighting fixture manufacturers might become interested in the product.

Last year jumper prices averaged 0.25 per pair. Jeff's variable costs ran around 0.10. Fixed costs were $600,000. Pricing below variable cost is not viewed as worthy of consideration by any producer.

Section_____

Name_____

Student Number_____

Assignment

A.   Before approaching the computer, answer the following questions.

1.   In what type of market environment (pure competition, monopoly, etc.) does Jeff's compete? Explain your reasoning.

_____

_____

_____

_____

2.   What should the industry demand curve look like? (Draw it in the block on the right.)

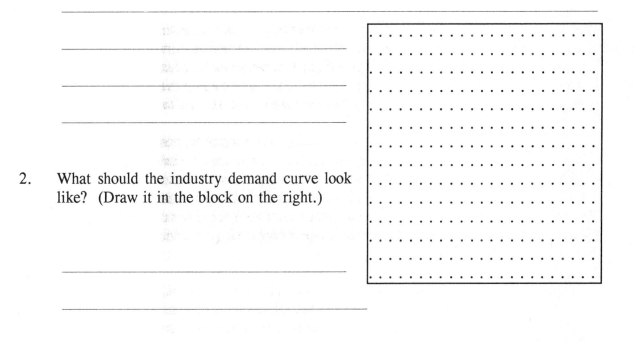

_____

_____

_____

3.   How should Jeff's sales respond to changes in its price?

_____

B. Select Marketing to Organizations from *The MART's* menu and complete the following exercises.

1. Run the *industry analysis*, trying various prices covering the relevant range. Try enough prices to get a solid feeling for the shape of the demand curve. Record the results below.

Price	Industry Quantity (millions)	Industry Total Revenue (millions)
0.60	_____	_____
_____	_____	_____
_____	_____	_____
_____	_____	_____
0.20	_____	_____
_____	_____	_____
_____	_____	_____
0.10	_____	_____

2. Run the *company analysis*. Try several prices below and above the "recent price". Complete the following table.

Prevailing price indicated was _____

Jeff's Price	Industry Price	Market Share	Unit Sales (millions)	Jeff's Sales($) (millions)	Contribution($) (millions)
0.60	____	_____	_____	_____	_____
____	____	_____	_____	_____	_____
____	____	_____	_____	_____	_____
____	____	_____	_____	_____	_____
0.20	____	_____	_____	_____	_____
____	____	_____	_____	_____	_____
____	____	_____	_____	_____	_____
0.10	____	_____	_____	_____	_____

Section_____   Name_____

                                            Student Number_____

3.   Plot the demand curves for all GG manufacturers (industry demand curve) and for Jeff's
      on a piece of graph paper, or in the block below.

      Allowing for random fluctuations built into the model, does this bear out your
      expectations recorded above (A.2 and A.3)?

      _____

      _____

4.   Both curves show a sharp bend or inflection.
      Are these caused by the same factor(s)?

      _____

      _____

      _____

      _____

      _____

IV Evaluating Opportunities

A marketer will, hopefully, be presented with more than one opportunity. All may appear attractive, taken individually. The marketer must evaluate the set and choose from among them.

If the alternatives are very similar, the estimated dollar profit may be an adequate basis for choice. If they are significantly different, they are likely to entail different levels of risk and the state of the environment may differentially affect their relative desirability. In such instances, *expected value analysis* is appropriate.

Multiple criteria. The decision-maker may wish to consider factors other than expected profit or return on investment (ROI). Perhaps social or environmental impacts of the alternatives differ significantly in ways which defy quantification in dollar terms. An analytic technique capable of incorporating multiple criteria is needed. An approach to this type of problem is included here.

The following cases will help you to understand methods for handling these more complex decision situations. They range in scope from a major regional bakery to a problem facing a student who represents his business school on a campus committee.

12 Bob's Bakery

Tim Beazley, marketing manager for breads at Bob's Bakery faced a series of decisions. Through trade journals and from their own kitchens, the bakery had come up with four types of bread that Tim could add to the line. The cost of producing and introducing a new line of bread on a trial basis ranged from a low of $69,000 to a high of $309,000, depending on the amount of promotion and advertising support the bread received. He felt that the low cost of product trial negated the need for research. It was cheaper to introduce the bread and flop in the market place, than spend money on research that was probably right, but could be wrong.

Bob Tuzo was the son of a wealthy businessman when his dad bought a small bakery in 1921. The father had renamed it Bob's Bakery after his young son Bob. Bob joined the firm in 1935 and worked his way up to president by 1950. As general manager and then president, Bob oversaw the expansion of the firm into two nearby counties. Through the fifties, sixties and seventies the firm prospered. However, the nature of the bakery business in the seventies and eighties changed in three ways.

Industry Developments

Consolidation

First, firms began to acquire other firms, or merge with them in order to gain market share and strength in the marketplace. The elimination of competitors and the economies of scale allowed the remaining companies to maintain profits. The result was that two bakeries now shared the Tri-County market between them. Their competitor, Central Bakery, was in turn owned by another large bakery in Chicago. This other bakery was, in turn, owned by a London based conglomerate called Simpson Inc., which was busily purchasing bakery operations world wide. Simpson viewed the baking industry as a growth market and was willing to pump a large part of its extensive cash reserves into developing their markets. Compared to this Goliath, Bob's Bakery was just the proverbial David with a slingshot, hoping speed and agility would be on its side.

Private Brands

The second major change was the growth of private label brands. The bread was produced by the bakeries and sold by the retailers under their own brand name. Private label bread is usually sold at or near cost, thus undercutting the price of the bakery's own branded breads substantially. A loaf of private label white bread could cost as little as $0.69, while a loaf of Bob's white bread sold for $1.29. As a consequence, Bob's was losing market share at a rapid rate. While Bob's supplied about 20% of the private label bread, it did not actively pursue this market, since profits tended to be minimal. On the other hand, Central pursued the private label market. Their strategy was to become partners with the grocery stores, supplying the private label brands while the stores gave Central's branded products preferred shelf space, thus squeezing Bob's products off the shelf.

Consumer Preferences

The third change was in consumers' tastes. There had been a slow but steady shift away from white bread, toward whole wheat or brown breads. The in-store bakeries were producing fresh-baked breads to compete in this market. Central was also introducing new breads. Bob's, however, was trying to be the market leader. Management felt that Bob's superior quality image and production capabilities gave them a competitive edge.

Decision Situation

Tim had been hired to spearhead the line expansion. He had narrowed the possibilities down to four new specialty breads (described below). He could introduce them all, or only some of them. He didn't plan to do any research, but, given the information from the trade journals, and the firm's past experience with similar products, he felt he could judge the probabilities of the market sales potential for each option. The basic decision for each bread was whether to introduce it, and if so, whether the bread should be supported by extensive promotion and advertising.

Tim decided to use expected value analysis to evaluate the potential profitability of each option as the first step in the decision process. This method of analysis also permits him to determine the value of (research) information in reducing uncertainty about the environment.

Brand Introductions

The cost of putting a new bread on the market included $4,000 to develop the bag and packaging, $700 for shelf talkers — those little flaps of cardboard that hang from the edge of the shelf announcing the presence of a new loaf of bread, $3,000 to $5,000 for 3 to 5 test runs in the bakery to ensure that the bread could be made correctly, and another $1,000 to produce free samples which were sent out to grocery outlets. This brought the fixed costs of development to $8,700 – $10,700.

Driver Salespersons

Bread is ordered by the drivers who are responsible for maintaining a good supply of fresh bread on the store shelves allocated to their bakery. If bread is on the shelf too long, the drivers return it to the bakery's Thrift Store, where it is sold at cost to consumers. Retailers are given a full credit for these returns.

Since the drivers are paid on a commission basis, it is important to them that they only stock fast moving, successful breads; they are penalized if their rate of returned "stales" is too high. The amount of unsold bread is, therefore, very low, no matter how unsuccessful an introduction may be. The drivers simply stop ordering it. In fact, if the drivers decide a new bread is not likely to survive, they could prematurely kill it by stopping all orders. As one driver put it, "It's a battlefield out there. We are constantly fighting with Central and the retailers for shelf space and I can't waste valuable shelf space on a loser."

Costs and Revenues

For an unsuccessful bread Tim could expect 40% returns, half of which would be sold in the Thrift Stores. (Product not moved through the Thrift Stores is, eventually, disposed of as animal feed at no net return.) Production costs are approximately $0.30 per loaf. For every thousand loaves placed on store shelves, they can expect to incur $60 in wasted production costs (400 X 0.5 X $.30).

However, the average contribution of the 60% or more sold by retailers is 45% to 50% of selling price for specialty breads. This means that a thousand loaves generate $270 – $300 in contribution toward overhead and profit. Subtracting the $60 lost due to "stales," even a loser brings in $210 to $240 per thousand loaves shipped. A winner brings in between $400 and $450.

Procedure

Tim generally knows within six weeks whether a new bread is a success, or not. He usually leaves the bread on the shelves in some stores for another six weeks, in order to see if sales might turn around. If sales were still disappointing after 12 weeks, the brand was withdrawn.

Actions and Outcomes

Product Alternatives

Tim is actively considering four alternatives. All are *specialty* breads which were selected as responsive to societal trends at the consumer level.

Date and Walnut. This is a light brown, sweet tasting bread with dates and walnuts throughout. Tim sees it consumed as toast for breakfast and with coffee or tea in the afternoon. The market potential is not large because of the special consumption situations, but he feels there is a 60% chance the medium level market sales potential exists for the bread. He gives a 30% chance there will be a low level of market sales potential, and a 10% chance of a high level of market sales potential.

Multigrain. This bread is designed to appeal to the health conscious adult consumer looking for a new taste and texture in their bread. This is a growing market and Tim assigns probabilities of 30%, 50% and 20% to there being a low, medium or high market sales potential for this bread.

Lite Bread. This bread was originally to be introduced as a diet bread, but the regulatory agency says that any product labelled "diet" has to have at least 25% fewer calories than the regular product. That is difficult to do with bread and have it appeal to a large market.

Instead, Tim is introducing a "lite" bread. This restricts the bread's potential appeal, but he still feels this bread has a fair chance of making it big. Consumers have been responding well to lite products, and the bread would likely be consumed by all age groups over many consumption situations. He assigned values of 10%, 40% and 50% of there being low, medium and high market sales potential.

Oat Bran. The marketplace has recently been inundated with oat bran products. Donut shops are selling oat bran donuts and muffins. Small retail bakeries are selling oat bran breads. As yet none of the large bakeries has introduced the product. Tim sees this as a fad bread, with a life span of three to five years. But while the fad lasts there is tremendous potential. He estimates there is a 70% chance that this is a high sales market, 25% it is a medium sales market, and only 5% that it is a low sales market.

Actions

Tim can choose from among three actions for each brand. First, he can *decide not to introduce* it. This action would have an expected payoff of $0. If he does introduce the brand, he can choose between two levels of promotional support. He can give a new bread *minimal support*, which includes the shelf talkers at $700, mentioned earlier, and newspaper advertising announcing the new bread. A large advertisement in the dailies costs them about $60,000.

Strong Support. If Tim decides to give a new brand extensive advertising and promotional support he will spend about $200,000 on T.V. and newspaper advertising. In addition, he will spend another $100,000 on direct mail campaigns, couponing, premiums to the drivers, bag collection contests, driver contests, cross promotion with other manufacturers, and public relations efforts.

States of Nature And Outcomes

Tim's estimates are summarized in Table 4. We will explain the table using the low market sales potential situation.

Table 4 Estimates Outcomes of Introducing a Brand

	Low Market Sales Potential		Medium Market Sales Potential		High Market Sales Potential	
	Weak Support	Strong Support	Weak Support	Strong Support	Weak Support	Strong Support
Loaves sold in four week period, in thousands (A)	7	10	21	30	70	100
Periods (B)	3	3	39	39	39	39
Revenue after stales per thousand loaves (C)	$210	$210	$400	$400	$450	$450
Total Revenue (A*B*C)	$4,410	$6,300	$327,600	$468,000	$1,228,500	$1,755,000
Development costs	$9,000	$9,000	$9,000	$9,000	$9,000	$9,000
Introduction	$60,000	$300,000	$60,000	$300,000	$60,000	$300,000
Contribution	-$64,590	-$302,700	$258,600	$159,000	$1,159,500	$1,446,000

The cost of introducing any of the four alternatives is, basically, the same. What differs is the chances of there being a particular level of market sales potential. A *low* market sales potential means that up to 10,000 loaves per month could be sold. If there is little advertising and promotional support, then Tim expects only 70% of the market potential (or 7,000 loaves every four weeks) would be sold. Strong support would result in sales of the full 10,000.

With a contribution margin of $210 per thousand loaves, a three period market trial generates a contribution of $4,410 toward overhead and profits. Given development costs averaging about $9,000 and advertising costs of $60,000, the total payoff is a loss of $64,590. With strong advertising and promotional support the full market potential of 10,000 loaves would likely be realized, contributing $6,300. However, after the $309,000 development and introduction costs are subtracted, the total payoff is a loss of about $303,000.

Assignment

Tim has several questions in mind as he turns to the computer to run the Expected Value program. He assumes the high potential breads are the ones he should introduce first, but is this true? The firm has a policy that a bread must be expected to contribute $200,000 over three years before it can be introduced. Do all of these breads qualify? Which breads should he introduce with the strong promotional support? Would the investment of $10,000 – $15,000 to determine the actual states of market sales potential be worth the cost?

Bob's Bakery is depending on its marketing expertise to compete effectively with Central and the retail stores. The key factor will be the effective introduction of new breads over the next couple of years. Tim knows they will only have one chance as he starts his analysis.

NOTE: Tim has three actions he can take: do not introduce the product, weak support and strong support. There are three hypothesized states, low, medium and high market sales potential. The payoff is $0 in all three states if the product is not introduced.

Assignment

Select Analyzing Market Opportunities from *The MART's* menu and complete the following.

1. Fill in the following table.

Bread	Action	Expected Value	Expected Value of Perfect Information
Date and Walnut	1	_____	
	2	_____	_____
	3	_____	
Multigrain	1	_____	
	2	_____	_____
	3	_____	
Lite Bread	1	_____	
	2	_____	_____
	3	_____	
Oat Bran	1	_____	
	2	_____	_____
	3	_____	

2. Do you think Tim should conduct research to obtain estimates of the market sales potential? Why or why not?

    _____

    _____

    _____

3. Explain how expected value under certainty may be higher than expected value under uncertainty.

_____

_____

_____

_____

4. For Multigrain the expected payoffs are all almost the same. Since it clearly pays to introduce the product, and the expected payoff is the same for either alternative if the product is introduced, is there any reason to bother doing research?

_____

_____

_____

5. How do the results change if Tim assumes a five year (65 period) payoff period?

_____

_____

_____

6. What are the weaknesses of this analysis?

_____

_____

_____

7. What kind of marketing strategy is Central pursuing? How is it developing strength in the market to compete with **Bob's** Bakery and with the retailers?

_____

_____

_____

8. Where do Bob's Bakery, Central and the retailers get their power in the market?

_____

_____

_____

9. In the long run, which bakery do you feel will likely be most profitable? Why?

_____

_____

_____

10. Tim has to market the new products to consumers and to retailers. What other group does he have to sell on the new brand(s)? What tools does he have available?

_____

_____

_____

13 Decisions Involving Multiple Criteria

Return on Investment (ROI) and expected value are, essentially, one dimensional approaches to evaluating a decision. In many instances, this will be completely satisfactory. In others several criteria must be considered simultaneously and a different approach is warranted.

For example, suppose two new product proposals are under consideration. Proposal A promises to produce a ROI of 13%, and is a premium product that can be expected to improve the image of all items sold under the family brand. It can be brought to market using the firm's present capabilities. Proposal B will produce a ROI of 11% and will not have the premium image of Product A. It will capitalize on existing capabilities to a degree, but will also require the firm to develop technological competence which will be a major asset in serving markets of the twenty first century. The required technology is within the state of the art and the related costs have been factored into the calculation of the ROI for the project.

This little example involves balancing variables that defy quantification. How do we analyze ROI and improved image and positioning for conditions expected in the distant future at the same time?

One way is to form a matrix as shown in Table 5. First, the variables to be considered are listed down the left hand side. Next, we rate those variables according to their importance to our organization. These ratings may be given by a single individual, or they may result from a consensus of executive opinion. If similar problems are a recurring event, they may be prescribed as a matter of organizational policy. It is easier to understand if these are normalized or scaled as a set of decimal fractions totalling to 1.0, but this is not necessary. (*The MART* will normalize the values for you, whatever values you choose to use.)

Next we rate each alternative on each dimension. Again, we can use any scale we wish as long as we are consistent. It is usual for higher values to indicate more favorable ratings. Next, we multiply the importance by the rating for each dimension and sum over the dimensions to get a score for each alternative. The alternative with the highest score is the most desirable.

Table 5 Sample problem

	Importance	Alternative Project A	Project B
ROI	.35	9	7
Improve Image of Product Line	.15	8	0
Utilizes Present Resources	.20	6	5
Position for the Future	.30	1	9
		—	—
Alternative's Score		5.85	6.15

The analysis need not be employed mechanically. Among its greatest virtues is pointing out the consequences of our judgments as to the importance of the variables and the ratings of the alternatives. We can change these and gauge the impact of the change on the outcome. However, one must be careful not to fall into the trap of just cooking the figures until they justify a decision already made.

14 Roth's Ruminations

Clive Roth made his money in the old fashioned way, he inherited it. Shortly before graduating from Brantford State, he had come into a considerable sum of money from the estate of his maternal grandmother. The amount was not enough to allow Clive to live entirely on the income. However, it was sufficient to alter his approach to the job market significantly.

Clive was a mature student who had worked for a number of years before entering the university and had held several responsible positions. Having always wanted to be his own boss, he had jumped at the chance to buy a paint and wallpaper store franchise with very little down payment, the original owner taking back a note for most of the purchase price.

This venture had proved to be a disaster. Only an unexpected upturn in remodeling activity in the area had allowed Clive to unload the store without taking a major loss. As a result of this experience he had decided he needed to develop an understanding of the esoteric terms his accountant was always throwing around, like "cash flow" and "negative net worth," and entered the university's Business School.

Opportunities

Clive was still interested in being his own boss. As a result of his grandmother's largess and his business degree, he felt able to "buy a job," if an opportunity could be found, rather than looking for one with someone else. After looking around and contacting several business brokers, Clive had identified three opportunities which he was actively considering.

Insta Maid provided contract housecleaning and home care services. It was viewed as highly successful. The firm's clients were largely employed in city government, the university and commercial establishments, so its revenues were pretty much unaffected by economic fluctuations. There were rumors, however, that Insta Maid's exceptional profitability was due to the fact that many of its part time employees were illegal immigrants who were paid less than minimum wage. This might have been sour grapes. However, a quick check with some clients revealed that, in most instances, one member of the two-women teams did all of the talking.

Casa Ruiz was a Mexican fast food restaurant franchised by a regional chain with an offering similar to the major national Taco chains. It was the only restaurant in the city offering any form of Mexican food, yet its growth had languished after an initial booming

72

success. As a result of slow growth, the asking price seemed right, if it could be gotten back on track. Yet, one of the major Mexican food franchises had, allegedly, looked at Brantford, decided its tastes in food were a bit conservative, and located elsewhere in the region. If Clive purchased Casa Ruiz he could expect some management assistance from the franchising firm, but would have to comply with its operating procedures.

Brantford Gifts seemed to Clive to have a split personality. During the summer it featured better souvenir items, targeting the vacationers thronging to the shores of Lake Brant. It stocked these items in both the main shop and an "annex" located in the lobby of the Lakeshore Hotel. Over 80% of summer sales come from the latter, which was open from May 15 to September 15. During the remainder of the year, the main store emphasized upscale gifts, china, crystal and silver flatware. Profitability was only average. Clive had some ideas for reorganizing the business that he felt would really improve its performance.

Criteria

Clive had worked out pro forma statements for each of the businesses and, using expected value calculations, determined his probable ROI. However, he wanted to consider other factors in arriving at a decision. If he were going to devote full time to his entrepreneurial venture, he would have to be able to pay himself a monthly salary. As a first approximation he figured each business could afford about what the present managers were being paid.

His experience with the paint store had left him highly risk averse, so he wanted to minimize his possible losses if his purchase did not work out. He wasn't a bleeding heart, but he, also, didn't want to exploit his community or the environment. He gave considerable importance to acting in a socially responsible manner.

Finally, upon reflection, Clive accepted the fact that his failure with the paint store had been due to his lack of knowledge about decorating, as well as to his lack of managerial skills. He felt that any new business he undertook should be one to which he could bring some expertise acquired through work experience, or university education.

Clive wanted to bring all of these factors to bear on his choice, yet, all were measured in different dimensions. In some instances large numbers were good and in others, such as maximum loss, large numbers were bad. Some, such as acting in a socially responsible manner, had no natural units of measurement.

To overcome these difficulties, he decided to give the various criteria ratings according to their importance to him. Then he rated the three alternatives on each of the dimensions, using a ten point scale. High numbers would indicated favorable values, so that a 10 would indicate both the highest possible ROI and the lowest loss.

After considerable effort Clive arrived at the ratings shown in Table 6.

Table 6 Clive Roth's Alternatives

	Importance	Insta Maid	Alternative Casa Ruiz	Brantford Gifts
Expected ROI	8	9	6	8
Maximum Loss	9	10	7	5
Salary	7	4	8	6
Socially Responsible	4	2	10	8
Independence	9	8	6	10
Have Expertise	5	3	10	9

Assignment

Choose the Spreadsheet model from *The MART's* menu and answer the following questions. If you have not read the description of the Spreadsheet model, you should do so. (p. 15)

1. Do you agree with Clive that multiple criteria should be considered in his decision? Why isn't expected ROI sufficient, since that is the variable we usually think of maximizing?

    _____

    _____

2. The maximum possible loss and the associated probability were, or could have been, included in the derivation of expected ROI. Is including it as a separate criterion justified?

    _____

    _____

3. Which alternative should Clive choose, given his ratings?

    _____

4. Which would he have chosen, based only on expected ROI?

    _____

5. Which would he have chosen if he viewed all criteria as equally important?

    _____

6. The course of action selected in 3, above, might have neither the highest expected ROI nor the greatest salary figure. Is this useful information in and of itself? How could it be useful?

_____

_____

7. Suppose social responsibility had been his greatest concern, say an importance score of 10. Which alternative would then be chosen?

_____

15 Campus Computer Committee

Fred Kratzner had been appointed as the business school's student representative to the Campus Computer Committee. The committee was in the process of choosing a replacement for the university's aging mainframe. Fred didn't really relate well to computers and had taken the appointment to advance his true interest, campus politics.

Fred took his responsibility seriously. Each member of the committee had received about a ton of information describing the different models competing for their favor. Fred had read it all, learned more than he had ever wanted to know about computers, and still felt lost. He tried talking to various faculty members. The computer types spouted off things about giga bytes and nano seconds and left him no better off than he had been before. Most of the others mumbled nearly incomprehensible platitudes that convinced him they were as much in the dark as he.

As the time to stand up in public and voice the business student's view approached, Fred reached a decision. He would limit his consideration to those attributes he, personally, understood, which was a very limited set, indeed. He wrote them down and then rated them on a ten point scale according to what he believed to be their importance to the average business student. He then scored the packages proposed by the competing manufacturers on each dimension, using a scale on which nine was the most favorable rating.

Fred's procedure resulted in the data shown in Table 7. Proposals are identified by code names assigned by the director of computing services.

Table 7 Ratings of Competing Proposals

		Proposal		
	Importance	I-beam	Decider	Cybele
Speed	3	3	6	6
Memory	3	6	3	9
Workstations Supported	4	5	6	2
Word Processor	7	8	3	8
Other Software	5	7	8	9
Cost	2	2	9	3
Ease of Learning New System	6	7	9	4
User Friendly	6	9	5	6

Assignment

Choose the Spreadsheet model from *The MART's* menu and answer the following questions. If you have not read the description of the Spreadsheet model, you should do so. (p. 15)

1. Which proposal would Fred favor based on the ratings in Table 7?

    _____

2. Would his decision change if the importance of cost had been rated 7 instead of 2?

    _____

3. Which proposal would he choose if all attributes were seen as equally important?

    _____

4. Which proposal would win out if memory were the only criterion to be considered?

    _____

5. The I-beam and Cybele proposals both incorporated the Gateword wordprocessor. What impact would it have if this system became available for the Decider?

    _____

V Market and Sales Forecasting

Let's make a forecast. What will the weather be like a year from today? Chances are that, before answering the question, you would look out the window, or at least give a thought to today's weather. When we ask our classes this question, they always give the "same as today" kind of answer and look at us as if we are idiots. If today's weather is unseasonably nice, they may shade that down a little bit. Strangely, if it's unusually unpleasant outside, they almost never predict it will be nicer a year into the future. That must say something about human nature.

Actually, the "same as today" answer makes eminently good sense. It involves estimating the future by making the best use we can of the available information.

Our approaches to business and economic forecasting share this characteristic of using information about the past and present to predict the future. The techniques employed vary widely. Yet, they all belong to one of two categories: extrapolation or causal modeling (correlational analysis). These are described in the following sections. Next, we turn to a discussion of measures of forecast accuracy, or goodness of fit.

Extrapolation

Extrapolation assumes that the history of the series to be predicted, itself, contains information that is useful in estimating the future. For example, to predict sales we would look at the product's sales history to make our forecast. In its simplest form, we might just plot the values over time and use a ruler to draw in a line which we feel best represents the pattern, then project this to the future period for which we wish to make a forecast.

Moving beyond this simple approach, there are any number of methods, varying widely in sophistication, from which one might choose. We will consider two: regression and exponential smoothing.

Regression

Regression is simply fitting the line mentioned in an earlier paragraph using mathematics, instead of ruler and eyeball. It involves deriving a simple linear model of the form

$$y=a+bx$$

which best fits the data. The variable to be predicted, or dependent variable is *y*, say sales in units. *x* is the independent or predictor variable. In this use of regression the independent variable represents units of time. It can be actual calendar years, months, periods since some starting point or any other convenient measure. The only restriction is that each interval represents the same length of time. The time passing between 1978 and 1979 is the same as the time between 1972 and 1973. This is the interval data assumption.

As long as the interval assumption is observed, the particular scale chosen for the independent variable does not matter. The years 1971 through 1980 can be coded 1971, 1972 ... 1980, or 1, 2, ... 10 and you will get the same prediction for a future year.

The regression coefficient, *b*, is the change in the dependent variable for each unit change in the independent variable, say the change in sales with each passing year. The constant, *a*, is the *y* intercept, the value *y* would take on when *x* is equal to zero. The values for *a* and *b* are determined through what was once a tedious series of computations. Fortunately, the computer is ideally suited to that sort of drudgery and can handle large problems in fractions of a second.

Simple regression is applicable only in instances in which a linear model provides an acceptable fit to the data and in which it is reasonable to project that linear model into the future. If the series shows large and frequent changes in direction, or if the situation has changed to such a degree that a model based on the past would not logically be expected to predict the future (maybe a competitor has introduced a new and superior product), then some other approach is appropriate.

Exponential Smoothing

There are a number of techniques for handling these more complex forecasting problems. One of the most common, due to its simplicity, is exponential smoothing. It uses the model shown below. We have presented it in the context of sales forecasting, but it can be applied to any time series.

$$Forecast_{(t+1)} = \alpha * Sales_t + (1 - \alpha) * Forecast_t$$

The forecast for the next period, *(t + 1)*, is the sum of two terms: (a) sales in the current period multiplied by the smoothing constant, α, and (b) the forecast for the current period multiplied by *(1 - α)*.

It may seem odd that our forecast is based on a previous forecast: a prediction based on a prediction. Think about it. The forecast for period *t* was based on sales in *(t - 1)* and the forecast for *(t - 1)*. The forecast for *(t - 1)* was derived from sales in *(t - 2)* and the forecast for *(t - 2)*, etc. Ultimately, the predictions are based on the product's entire sales history.

Like the proverbial elephant, exponential smoothing never forgets. As we go backwards each period has an exponentially declining weight, hence the name.

α, which varies between zero and one (0.0 - 1.0), controls the degree to which current sales, as opposed to the longer sales history, influences our projections. At the extremes, if we set α to one, we ignore all past experience. A low value for α gives greater emphasis to earlier periods.

No method of extrapolation can predict or anticipate turning points in the series being monitored. The value of α chosen affects the rapidity with which the model responds to a change, after it has occurred. High values cause the model to respond rapidly, low values more slowly. High values would tend to perform better when the series changes sharply and frequently. This would make it seem that high values were always better. Unfortunately, high values cause the model to overreact to random fluctuations in the data.

There is no "correct" value for α. One normally tries a range of values and chooses the one which produces the most satisfactory projections. We have used the Mean Absolute Deviation (MAD) as a measure of forecast accuracy for exponential smoothing (below).

In case you're not already confused, let's complicate the situation a bit more. The value produced by the model shown above actually estimates the true state of the series at time t. If there are pronounced long term trends, seasonal, cyclical or other factors to be considered, more complex formulations are available. We leave it to the interested reader to consult more advanced works on forecasting.

Causal Modeling

In the approaches previously discussed, we looked to the history of the series to be predicted for information to be used in predicting future values of that same series. We used the sales history to predict future sales. In causal modeling, or correlational approaches, we try to find other variables that vary, or correlate with the variable of interest and that can be used to make predictions for the future. We might use an estimate of population size to predict sales of some basic food item, such as bread.

At the outset, we should say that, though we have used the term causal modeling, causation lies within the observer, not the modeling. The statistical routine, simple regression, merely takes the values of the two series and gives us a mathematical statement of the relationship between them. This statement only means that the two series tend to move together in a certain manner, or correlate. It doesn't imply that there is a causal relationship at work. For example, wags have identified significant relationships between the movement of stock prices and both the outcome of the Superbowl and movements up and down of women's hemlines. One is hard pressed to find any causal mechanism at work in these instances.

As in extrapolation, we are projecting the past into the future. When extrapolating we are assuming that there are meaningful patterns or trends in the history of a series, such as sales, that can be expected to continue. In causal modeling we attempt to find *relationships* among variables that can be expected to continue to exist. If population size predicted bread sales in the past, our assumption is that it will continue to do so. This assumption is at the heart of our forecasting efforts. It is also partly responsible for some notable failures.

Independent Variables

The simple regression routine provided uses the same model and requires the same assumptions as those discussed in the previous section. The variable we want to predict is y, our dependent variable. The independent variable is one which we believe will be a useful predictor. We do have more confidence in the resulting model if there is some natural, or logical relationship between the dependent variable and its predictor.

One other factor must be considered in choosing from among candidate independent variables. We must know the value the independent variable will have in the period for which we want a forecast *at the time* we are making our prediction. This can be a problem. Suppose we wanted to make a forecast of sales of fuel efficient cars and found a strong relationship with the current — spot — price of oil. That might not be much help. Oil prices have varied more wildly and have been more difficult to predict than car sales in recent decades.

All is not lost. Many of the dependent variables you might wish to use are either easy to predict, or are factors for which reliable estimates are readily available. Populations change slowly in the short- and mid-term and government demographers' projections are available, even for relatively small areas. Government, major banks, trade associations, investment services, and many others churn out masses of economic predictions. The individual forecaster's task is not finding an estimate, but choosing from among those at hand.

Lead-Lag Relationships

Lastly, the forecaster's dream, the lead–lag relationship. Suppose oil prices affected fuel efficient car sales a year or eighteen months out, rather than in the current period. Then we don't have to worry about predicting oil prices. The value is a matter of record well in advance of the period for which a forecast is needed.

Lead – lag relationships suggest an advantage of causal modeling over extrapolation. We can anticipate changes in the direction of the series we wish to project, whereas extrapolation can only respond, once a change has occurred. Suppose we wished to predict sales of crayons. Sales of crayons are very strongly related to the size of the elementary school population. All those who will enter school for the next five or six years are now born. By monitoring birth rates and births, we could anticipate changes in crayon sales well in advance.

Think

Let us close this section with a plea. Since students hate the word theory, let us suggest that you should have some good, logical reason why a relationship should exist, before using it in your forecasts. If you don't, you are in danger of being left flapping in the wind when a spurious relationship ceases to hold.

You may ask how we reconcile this with extrapolation, in which time, itself, is the independent or predictor variable. Simply put, we don't. In extrapolation time is merely a surrogate for some other unknown, and perhaps unknowable factor. For example, we might find time serves as a surrogate for increasing population, income growth, or any of a number of other factors.

Significance

We can feed any two sets of numbers, even truly random numbers, into a regression routine and it will develop a regression model. The program is like a loyal, but not overly bright, dog. It will do its best, no matter how meaningless the result.

Similarly, assume we were to repeatedly pick numbers from each of two sets of random numbers. By sheer chance, some of our picks would show moderate to strong relationships in a regression, even though no real relationship exists.

If we are going to bet our businesses, or our careers on a model's predictions, we want some assurance that the relationship is at least stronger that we would find between two sets of randomly drawn numbers. Unfortunately, we can never say with absolute certainty that a model is "real." However, statistical theory lets us determine the likelihood of obtaining a particular model when there is, in fact, no relationship. The test of significance helps us make this assessment.

The "T" statistic is an indicator of the strength of the relationship which a regression represents. Larger values of "T" indicate stronger relationships. In the bad old days before computers, we calculated "T," and then went to a set of statistical tables to determine the significance level. In the forecasting package described below, the computer does the work of going to the tables for you. We present the "T" value simply because it is conventional to do so.

The significance level tells us the probability of obtaining the relationship we have observed, by chance, when, in fact, no real relationship exists. Since it is a probability statement, significance levels lie in the range 0.0 – 1.0. The smaller the number the stronger the relationship.

A significance value of 0.1 for a regression means there is one chance in ten (10 in 100) of finding a relationship as strong as the one we have observed by chance. A value of 0.5 would indicate we would find this strong a relationship by chance half the time, while 0.05 means it would only happen 5 times in 100. The value 0.000 sometimes confuses students. This is presented when the probability, after rounding, is less than 0.001.

Forecast Accuracy

In regression we have provided two measures of accuracy, or goodness of fit: Pearson Correlation and Mean Absolute Deviation (MAD). Only MAD is provided for Exponential Smoothing, since the Pearson Correlation is limited to linear relationships.

Pearson Correlation

The Pearson Correlation Coefficient, r, measures the strength of the relationship between two variables — the degree to which a linear model fits the observed data. It ranges from –1.0 to 1.0. A value of 1.0 would indicate a perfect positive relationship, i.e., as x increases y increases. A value of –1.0 indicates a perfect negative relationship. Values close to either extreme are equally good for forecasting. Values close to zero indicate weak relationships, or no association.

We, conventionally, look at the square of the correlation coefficient, r^2 (pronounced r square). This value indicates the proportion of the variation in one variable explained by the other. An r^2 of 0.5 between A and B indicates that 50% of the variation in B is explained by A, or, since the relationship is symmetrical, that 50% of the variation in A is explained by B.

Higher values of r^2 — and r — are, naturally, better. There are no hard and fast rules as to acceptable levels, it depends on the area being studied. Values of r^2 above 0.9 are frequently demanded by financial and economic forecasters, before the relationship is considered to be useful. Those working with human behavior would find values that large highly suspect, since they are accustomed to r^2's of 0.3 – 0.5, and below.

Mean Absolute Deviation (MAD)

Many will have previously encountered the Pearson Correlation Coefficient. The MAD is less well known, though it is much simpler to calculate. To determine MAD one merely takes the absolute value of the difference between the observed and predicted value for each observation. Add these up and divide by the number of observations and you have the MAD.

Unlike the correlation coefficient, the MAD has no fixed range. The lower bound is zero and the sky's the limit at the upper end. It's magnitude is affected by the scale of measurement as well as the fit of the model being tested. All that can be said is that, for any set of observations, smaller is better.

The Data Analysis and Forecasting Package

The MART contains an easy to use, but powerful, Data Analysis and Forecasting (DAF) package. It includes routines for extrapolating past data using either regression or exponential smoothing and for causal modeling using regression analysis. The data for any of the cases in this chapter can be loaded by making the appropriate selection from the DAF menu. The Data Management menu also offers users the opportunity to enter and edit their own data, save it to disk, and recall it at a later date for use in the statistical routines.

To use DAF, make the appropriate selection from the main menu. The program is completely menu driven. Simply follow the instructions that appear at the bottom of the screen.

Do not insert commas in numbers when entering or changing data. The computer will reject these as illegal input. When the computer displays a number, it will insert commas for ease of reading. Also you should not attempt to enter dollar signs, or other units. If you do, you will be severely beeped.

Some entries must be followed by pressing <Enter> (carriage return). Anytime nothing happens when you think you have provided the required input, press the <Enter> key.

If you enter your own data, we strongly suggest that you immediately save it to disk, even though you are sure you will never need it again. Remember what your mother always told you. "Better save than sorry." This will require having a formatted disk with space available before it is needed. Being certified paranoids, we would also recommend frequently making backup copies on a second disk.

Regression displays statistics not described in these instructions. They are additional tools for evaluating a regression, but are a little beyond most students in this course. We print these just in case you have the good common sense to hang onto the book and its disks for use in the future, after further preparation in statistics. The DAF package, alone, would cost several times what you paid for the book, if purchased in the software market.

A closing note on the exponential smoothing routine. As noted above, we have included a very simple smoothing model, because we feel this version is most appropriate for class use. The model makes a best estimate of the "true" value of the series after the last observation and takes that as its prediction for the next period. It will produce this same value regardless of the period for which you ask for a forecast.

16 L. Wetzel Blank Book

L. Wetzel, Inc. entered the twentieth century as a general purpose printing house, taking almost any sort of a job as it came. The firm continued in this mode until the early teens when it started emphasizing service to various levels of government. This proved to be a fortuitous choice and the contacts developed were to become extremely valuable. With the coming of WW I, federal government and armaments-related business was an absolute gold mine. They might as well have been printing money. However, this dried up and the firm suffered a radical drop in sales after the war ended.

The firm had a small financial printing operation. During the runaway financial markets of the roaring twenties, this division grew until it contributed 70% of sales and 88% of profits. Unfortunately, sales crashed, along with the markets, in twenty nine.

Wetzel's officers were left searching for a route to survival and growth. Having experienced the crashes in the defense and financial printing markets, they were inclined to turn to something steadier, if less spectacular.

The financial printing division had serviced the needs of banks for forms, ledgers, checks, deposit slips, etc. This was not as exciting or profitable as printing share certificates and prospectuses for new issues, but it was a lot more stable and it sustained the firm, in a scaled down form, during the dark days of the early thirties.

Sean Michaels, the president, had noted the rapidly growing tendency of individual Americans to own checking accounts that became apparent in the mid thirties. He decided that this offered just the sort of opportunity the firm needed for rapid, steady growth. The firm concentrated on meeting the growing demand by banks for checks for their retail customers. Today the firm has sales of over half a billion dollars, 85% coming from printing checks and related items. It enjoys over a 50% market share in its major lines and provides goods or services, of some sort, to over 90% of US banks.

Forecasting had not been a high priority item at Wetzel. It had consisted of merely predicting that next year's sales would be up or down by some amount over this year's, based on the marketing research director's gut feel. Senior management had grown increasingly dissatisfied with the results and had directed that more sophisticated approaches be explored.

Some navel contemplating, followed by a few quick plots indicated a relationship might exist between sales and total deposits in the banking system. The data illustrated below was assembled for use in developing a forecasting model. The square of total deposits has been

Table 8   Total US Bank Deposits and Wetzel Sales

Year	Deposits (billions)	Deposits Squared (billions)	Sales (Millions)
1925	53.1	2,819	142.9
1926	54.4	2,959	103.0
	...		
1990	2575.6	6,633,803	672.1
1991 est	2700.0	7,290,540	

included, since the plot of deposits and sales over time is decidedly nonlinear. Your mission, should you choose to accept it, is to see if this data can be useful in Wetzel's forecasting problem.

Section_____   Name_____

                     Student Number_____

Assignment

Use the DAF module to perform the following tasks. Choose Wetzel Blank Book from the DAF menu and complete the following exercises.

1. Develop a model to predict Wetzel's sales in 1991. Complete the following table. If an entry is not applicable, leave it blank. Try various smoothing constants and enter the results for the one you feel to be best. Develop regression models using total deposits and total deposits squared as the independent variable (IV).

Forecast Method	1991 Sales	r^2	MAD	Inter-cept (a)	Slope (b)	Smoothing Constant
Extrapolation: Regression						
Extrapolation: Smoothing						
Causal Modeling IV =						
Total Bank Deposits						
Total Deposits Squared						

2. Use the regression option to see if you can develop a model to make your own predictions

    a) of total deposits in 1991.

    _____

    b) of the square of total deposits in 1991.

    _____

91   *L. WETZEL BLANK BOOK*

3. Repeat 2, using the exponential smoothing option. Try different smoothing constants.

   a) total deposits in 1991.

   _____

   b) the square of total deposits in 1991.

   _____

4. Which technique works best for which variable? Why would this be so?

   _____

   _____

   _____

   _____

5. Write your regression model for predicting sales

   a) based on a measure of total deposits.

   _____

   b) by extrapolation.

   _____

17 Ol' Time Hardware

Ol' Time Hardware Inc. opened its first store in 1981 in Springfield. At the time, this store was viewed as an anachronism. In an age of self-service building supply stores, it was a real old fashioned hardware store. It offered full service, a wide assortment of difficult to obtain merchandise and friendly, competent advice. According to its owner, Jim Livingston, there was a substantial number of people out there who want to be able to buy a nail that wasn't in a plastic bubble pack.

Strategy

The original store had enjoyed steady, but unspectacular growth and Ol' Time had opened new stores in several communities in the surrounding area. Ol' Time's customers seemed to truly appreciate its offering and exhibited extremely high levels of loyalty. Prices were above those charged by the mass merchandisers, but the chain's patrons seemed to feel that the assortment, ability to buy one — or a few — of an item and friendly, personal service were worth the difference.

Two factors were critical to being able to offer these factors at affordable prices: inventory control and staffing. From the very beginning Jim, a computer nut, had invested heavily in inventory management programs that kept inventory investment to the bare minimum, given the breadth of assortment.

The stores were staffed with retired craftsmen, particularly those of the handyman sort. They worked for near minimum wage just to have something to do and make a little money to supplement their retirement income. Critics viewed this policy as exploitative, particularly since benefits were practically nonexistent. However, morale was high and the employees, truly, seemed to enjoy the opportunity to employ their knowledge to help patrons solve their problems. Some said they would have done the work for nothing, if necessary, because it beat "jest sittin' and rockin'."

Store Location Problem

Jim felt that it was time to consider additional store locations and was interested in expanding to other regions of the country. He had a nagging fear that he had just lucked out in picking Springfield and its surrounding cities for the original locations, and wanted to base future site selections on sounder analyses. Based on his experience to date, he knew that Ol' Time's sales were highly correlated with total hardware store sales in a community. He felt that hardware store sales were, in turn, very closely related to the size of the population and total and per capita retail sales.

Estimates of hardware sales were not available for many of the communities in which Jim might be interested, but information on population and retail sales was. If these were, as he believed, predictive of hardware sales, they would be useful in the site location process.

Livingston planned a two step process. To see if his hypothesis was viable without too large an expenditure of effort, Jim gathered data at the state level (Table 9) for a sample of

Table 9 Livingston's Data for Ten States

Popula-tion (000)	House-holds (000)	Retail Sales (000,000)	Per Capita Retail Sales	Hard-ware Sales (000)
9,024.0	3,299.7	$46,614.0	$5,165.6	$310,537
2,337.7	838.4	12,567.7	5,376.1	87,747
2,882.9	1,111.0	13,854.0	4,805.6	84,967
1,065.2	395.8	4,841.6	4,545.3	29,772
1,434.6	475.2	6,185.0	4,311.3	62,112
878.2	304.6	4,254.5	4,844.6	35,679
1,157.8	327.6	4,371.4	3,775.6	20,832
760.8	251.4	3,296.9	4,333.5	18,876
6,562.3	2,388.9	30,733.4	4,683.3	389,913
1,016.4	373.4	4,644.8	4,569.9	50,049

10 states. If useful relationships were found, he would expend the effort to assemble data on a larger sample of smaller areas.

Your assignment is to use the Data Analysis and Forecasting (DAF) module to assist Jim in his site selection task.

Assignment

Choose Data Analysis and Forecasting, then Data Management from *The MART's* menus. Enter the data in Table 9 as a new data set.

1. Complete the following table. If an entry is not applicable, leave it blank. (*Think*) Develop regression models using population, then total retail sales as the independent variable.

Forecast Method	r^2	MAD	Inter-cept (a)	Slope (b)	Smoothing Constant
Extrapo-lation: Regression					
Extrapo-lation: Smoothing					
Causal Modeling IV =					
Population					
Total Retail Sales					

2. What forecasting technique would you choose?

_____

3. Do population and hardware sales appear to be related?

_____

4. What is the nature of the relationship?

   _____

5. How strong is the relationship (if any)?

   _____

   _____

6. Do population and per capita retail sales appear to be related?

   _____

   _____

7. What is the nature of the relationship?

   _____

   _____

8. How strong is the relationship (if any)?

   _____

   _____

Assignment

Ol' Time Hardware (Assignment 2)

After the preceding analysis, Jim decided to continue the project and conduct the analysis at the county level for several states in which he was particularly interested. He also decided to see if the dollar value of building permits might be of predictive value. The data for a random sample of counties is illustrated below and is stored on the program disk. Load this data set using the DAF Data Management Menu.

Population (000)	Households (000)	Retail Sales ($000)	Hardware Sales ($000)	Total Income ($000)	Building Permits ($000)
45.4	16.2	316,911	2,638	415,836	3,159.1
76.6	27.9	431,643	3,081	788,706	3,886.9

Complete the following table. If an entry is not applicable, leave it blank. (*Think*) Develop regression models using each of the variables shown as the independent variable.

Forecast Method	r^2	MAD	Inter-cept (a)	Slope (b)	Smoothing Constant
Extrapo-lation: Regression					
Extrapo-lation: Smoothing					
Causal Modeling IV =					
Population					
Total Retail Sales					
Value Building Permits					

OL' TIME HARDWARE

1. What analytic technique did you use?

    _____

    _____

2. Are population and hardware sales related at the county level?

    _____

    _____

3. What is the nature of the relationship?

    _____

    _____

4. How strong is the relationship (if any)?

    _____

    _____

5. What would explain the difference between the results here and those in assignment A, above?

    _____

    _____

6. Can you find a better predictor at the county level?

    _____

    _____

18 Kinder Kottage

Leslie Williams, a senior marketing student at Commonwealth University, was reflecting upon her recent interview with Kinder Kottage, Inc. Kinder Kottage operated a chain of stores selling infant goods to the carriage trade. Historically, the chain had concentrated on durables. Recently, it had begun giving somewhat greater emphasis to nondurables including designer label socks, talcums and lotions imported from Paris, and hand embroidered sheets. The stores were located in suburbs throughout the Capitol City MSA.

Leslie had been impressed with the company's management and their plans for the future. However, in the following days she had begun to have second thoughts. Since the chain was totally dependent on items for infants, and had no plans for expansion beyond the Capitol City region, she decided to dig out data on the local birth rates. These are plotted in Figure VII. Hardly promising. The average number of children per family has declined from a baby boom high of 3.8 to around 1.6.

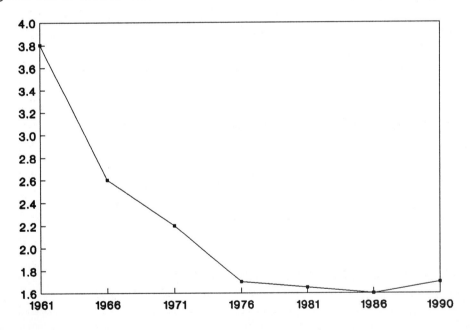

Capitol City is a demographic anomaly. It generally experiences the same trends as the country as a whole. However, the timing is often out of sync. For various reasons, turning points often lead or lag the national aggregates by as much as seven to ten years.

After a great deal of work with census, trade association, chamber of commerce and Kinder Kottage data, Leslie had put together the information illustrated below (Table 10). This data can be called from the DAF main menu. Playpens were chosen as representative of durables and lotions as indicative of nondurables. To ease comparisons, sales data for the two products have been converted to *sales indices* with 1965 as the base year. The fertility rate is, roughly, the average number of children per completed family.

Table 10 Sample of Leslie's Data

Year	Fertility Rate	Total Births	Lotion Sales	Playpen Sales
1955	3.5	3752.3	109.0	85.1
...				
1965	2.9	3415.3	100.0	100.0
...				
1990	1.6	3647.7	107.7	136.1
1991(est)	1.7	4049	?	?

Assignment

Choose Data Analysis and Forecasting from *The MART's* menu. Complete the following exercises.

1. Fill in the following tables. If an entry is not applicable, leave it blank. Try various smoothing constants and record the one you feel performs best. Develop regression models using total births as the independent variable (IV).

Forecasting Playpen Sales

Forecast Method	1991 Sales Playpens	r^2	MAD	Inter-cept (a)	Slope (b)	Smoothing Constant
Extrapo-lation: Regression						
Extrapo-lation: Smoothing						
Causal Modeling IV =						
Total Births						

Forecasting Lotion Sales

Forecast Method	1991 Sales Lotions	r^2	MAD	Inter-cept (a)	Slope (b)	Smoothing Constant
Extrapo-lation: Regression						
Extrapo-lation: Smoothing						
Causal Modeling IV =						
Total Births						

2.   Which technique worked best

    a. for playpens?

    _____

    b. for baby lotion?

    _____

3.   What is your forecasting model

    a. for playpens?

    _____

    b. for baby lotion?

    _____

4.   Assume playpens are representative of durables sales and baby lotion is representative of nondurables. Which category will experience the greatest rate of increase or decrease as the number of births increases?

    _____

    _____

    _____

5.   Based on what you know about changes in the family, can you think of an explanation of why the two categories differ?

    _____

    _____

    _____

6. The Census Bureau predicts that 4,309 children will be born in Capitol City in 1995. These predictions have proven highly reliable.

a. What is your prediction for sales of baby lotion in 1995?

_____

b. What is your prediction for sales of playpens in 1995?

_____

7. Would you continue to pursue the position if you were Leslie? Explain.

_____

_____

_____

_____

VI Marketing Arithmetic

Marketing is fun, right? Right. You don't have to worry about all those dumb numbers and stuff, right? Wrong! Marketers are just as concerned with "the numbers" as anyone else. These exercises will help you understand some calculations and a few of the relationships of concern to marketers. Try to focus on the information required for a calculation and what the results would mean to you as a manager. The computer will handle the drudgery of routine computation.

Markup Calculations

Markup is what it's all about. This is the amount added to the cost of producing or acquiring goods to cover selling expenses, overhead and administrative expenses and provide for some profit. If the item is sold the markup becomes the gross profit.

$$(1) \ Selling \ Price \ = \ Cost \ of \ Goods \ + \ Markup$$

Markups are usually expressed as a percentage of either selling price or of the cost of goods. In managing or evaluating markups it is important to understand the basis being used

$$(2) \ \% \ Markup \ on \ Selling \ Price \ = \ 100 \ X \ \frac{Dollar \ Markup}{Selling \ Price}$$

$$(3) \ \% \ Markup \ on \ Cost \ = \ 100 \ X \ \frac{Dollar \ Markup}{Cost}$$

in the calculation. (Markups based on cost are sometimes referred to as Markons.) Markup on Cost can take on any value. Since markup on selling price cannot exceed selling price, Markup on Selling Price cannot be greater than 100%.

Assume an item is purchased for $5.00 and sold for $10.00. The Markup on Cost is 100%. The Markup on Selling Price is 50%.

Since the two markups are both based on the terms in (1), it is a simple matter to convert from one to the other.

$$(4) \ \% \ Markup \ on \ Selling \ Price \ = \ 100 \ X \ \frac{\% \ Markup \ on \ Cost}{100 \ + \ \% \ Markup \ on \ Cost}$$

$$\text{(5)} \ \% \ \textit{Markup on Cost} = 100 \ X \ \frac{\textit{Markup on Selling Price}}{100 - \textit{Markup on Selling Price}}$$

Continuing the example, above

$$\% \ \textit{Markup on Selling Price} = 50 = 100 \ X \ \frac{100}{100 + 100}$$

$$\% \ \textit{Markup on Cost} = 100 = 100 \ X \ \frac{50}{100 - 50}$$

High markups are not necessarily good. They produce higher prices and, probably, result in lower unit sales.

Chain Discounts

Prices are frequently stated in terms of discounts from a retail selling price. The simplest type of chain discounts are the functional discounts allowed a channel member as compensation for the marketing functions performed. (Functional discounts are not legal in Canada.) Assuming the channel members adhere to the discount schedule and suggested price, the discount will constitute their Markup (on selling price) on the item.

For example, an item may have a suggested retail price of $2.00 with a discount of 40% for retailers and 25% for wholesalers. The retailer's cost is $1.20 [(1.0 - 0.4) X $2.00] and the Markup on Selling Price is $0.80 (0.4 X $2.00, or $2.00 - $1.20). The same $1.20 is, naturally, **the wholesaler's** selling price. The wholesaler's cost is $.90 [(1.0 - .25) X $1.20] and the Markup at wholesale is $0.30. The wholesaler could determine his cost in a single step by multiplying through by the chain of discounts. The wholesaler's cost is $2.00 X (1.0 - .4) X (1.0 - .25) = $0.90.

Some situations may involve larger numbers of discounts. Examples are endless, but might include such things as

Advertising Allowances: given to wholesalers and retailers to pay for ads they place for the manufacturer's product.

Cash Discounts: given to customers to encourage prompt payment of a bill.

Functional Discounts: (above).

Price Adjustments: used to make prices flexible while maintaining relatively constant list prices.

Push Money: (also called Spiffs). Given to a channel member to be passed on to that channel member's salespersons for pushing the manufacturer's products.

Stocking Allowances: given to channel members to encourage them to carry larger inventories of a manufacturer's product than they might otherwise stock. Also used to obtain greater than normal shelf space or more desirable shelf space.

Any series of discounts can be calculated as a simple chain multiplication, subtracting each discount (stated as a proportion) from 1.0. If the final price is $4.00 with a functional discount of 50%, an advertising allowance of 10% and the retailer is paying promptly to earn a cash discount of 2%, then the amount due on the invoice is

$$\$4.00 \ X \ (1.0 - 0.5) \ X \ (1.0 - 0.1) \ X \ (1.0 - 0.02) = \$1.67$$

The order in which the discounts are taken makes no difference, naturally.

Cash Discounts

It is normal for credit to be extended in business transactions. Cash discounts are granted to encourage prompt payment by one's customers. A cash discount is usually stated in the form 2/10 net 30. This indicates that the customer may take a 2% discount if the invoice is paid within 10 days. If the discount is not taken, the total is due at the end of 30 days.

The person offering a cash discount really wants it to be taken, so it is usually structured to make it prohibitively expensive not to do so. Even the one given in the preceding paragraph equates to an annual interest rate of 36%. How is that?

If the discount is not taken, one is paying 2% of the total for 20 (30 - 10) days of credit. Making the conventional assumption of a 360 day year, there are 18 (360/20) periods of that length per year in which the discount could be earned. Alternatively stated, one is paying 2% for the use of the money for one eighteenth of a year. The equivalent annual rate is 36%, a little better than you are earning on your savings account. If necessary, it would be wise to borrow at market rates to avoid missing a discount of that magnitude.

Markdowns

You can't win them all. Some of what's marked up will be marked down. If merchandise hasn't sold, it probably won't move any better after gathering dust on the shelves for a while longer. The ski caps that haven't sold in January won't sell any better in July.

Computer Models

The computer models for this section are completely self prompting. Simply press enter if a value isn't available to you. The computer will complete its calculations when enough information has been provided. If you make an incorrect entry, just reenter the correct data when given the opportunity.

In many instances the computer models will recalculate some values when new data is entered that replaces an existing figure. In general, only those values that naturally follow will be recalculated. For example, in the markup model, you might change a channel member's selling price. Say the channel member is a wholesaler. The retailer's cost will be reset, but not the retail selling price. That must be changed by a subsequent entry.

19 Far North Manufacturing

Far North Manufacturing, Inc., markets a line of weatherproofing products under the Stormaway brand name. The majority of its products are manufactured in Far North's own plants. The balance, primarily items based on various applications of adhesive tapes, are obtained from outside suppliers. These items are not particularly profitable, but Far North's management feels it is necessary to be able to supply its dealers with a full line of products.

Far North's products are used primarily by do-it-yourselfers retrofitting existing homes. The balance are purchased by new home builders and renovation contractors.

Far North was recently approached by an inventor touting a vastly improved threshold strip for sealing the bottom of a home's exterior doors. It could be installed easily in either new or existing structures and formed a near perfect seal against drafts. Testing seemed to confirm the claim of a nearly unlimited life with no need for replacement of any components. Durability was a major selling point, but it also meant there would be no lucrative aftermarket in parts. Far North had decided to introduce the item and agreed to pay the inventor a license fee of $0.25 per item.

Production estimated manufacturing costs of $8.00 per unit for the threshold strip. Far North's policy was to add 100% to the direct costs of an item to arrive at a selling price.

Far North sold its products through building supply wholesalers who expected a markup of 19% of selling price. They, in turn, sold to building supply stores and hardware stores who added on a markup of 32% of selling price.

Assignment

1. Use the Markup program to complete the following table.

	Manufacturer	Wholesaler	Retailer
Cost - $			
Selling Price - $			
Gross Profit - $			
Markup on Cost - %			
Markup on SP - %			

It turned out that the inventor was *really* enthusiastic about his threshold strip. So enthusiastic, in fact, that it seems that he had already sold exclusive rights to Snow Belt Industries prior to approaching Far North. Snow Belt has "generously" agreed to license its rights to Far North for $0.75 per unit. (The inventor decided the best way to cope with winter was from a South Pacific island republic whose claims to fame were great weather and absolutely no extradition treaties. He, obviously, will not be paid royalties.)

2. What effect does this have on prices?

	Manufacturer	Wholesaler	Retailer
Cost - $			
Selling Price - $			
Gross Profit - $			
Markup on Cost - %			
Markup on SP - %			

3. What if actual manufacturing costs turn out to be $8.13? (Royalties must still be paid.) Complete the following table.

	Manufacturer	Wholesaler	Retailer
Cost - $			
Selling Price - $			
Gross Profit - $			
Markup on Cost - %			
Markup on SP - %			

4. Far North's corporate jet has ended up costing about twice the expected amount. To cover this unexpected expense, Far North's management has decided to change their markon to 105%. What impact will this have on prices throughout the channel, assuming no other policy changes? (Manufacturing costs remain at $8.13.)

	Manufacturer	Wholesaler	Retailer
Cost - $			
Selling Price - $			
Gross Profit - $			
Markup on Cost - %			
Markup on SP - %			

5. Markup pricing is quite common. What is your opinion of this approach? What does it neglect?

_____

_____

_____

A mass merchandiser has approached Far North about buying a large quantity of threshold strips directly, rather than from wholesalers. It proposes selling them at retail for $25.49, after taking a markup of 23%.

6.   What will Far North's selling price be if it accepts this arrangement? (*Hint:* To eliminate a channel level set the markup and profit for that member to zero, or use any two adjacent columns and ignore the headings.)

	Manufacturer	Wholesaler	Retailer
Cost - $			
Selling Price - $			
Gross Profit - $			
Markup on Cost - %			
Markup on SP - %			

20 Consolidated Dry Goods

Mark Waddell is a men's sleepware buyer for Consolidated Dry Goods, a Major Department store chain on the East Coast. Having noted the success of casual shorts and other sportswear in wild Hawaiian patterns, he has decided to capitalize on this fad by introducing a line of similarly patterned men's pajamas. The design work has been completed and a name selected: UGLI JAMS. Mark is preparing to discuss manufacturing specifications with a Korean Manufacturer. Since the product will be made to Consolidated's order, it will be manufactured on a cost plus basis.

Consolidated will have men's pajamas priced at $14.99, $17.99, $19.99 and $24.99 next season. Since UGLI JAMS are viewed as something of a fad item, Mark envisions pricing them at the upper price point. Consolidated's management will expect a markup of 30% on the selling price. The manufacturer is expected to ask for a markup on his selling price of between 14.7% and 15.3%.

Use the markup model to answer the following questions. (*Hint:* Set the wholesalers' markup at zero.)

Assignment

1. What is the largest amount that will be available for the manufacturer to spend producing each item?

    _____

    What is the smallest?

    _____

2. Suppose Waddell targeted the $19.99 price point. In what range would manufacturing costs have to fall?

    _____

    What range would apply to the $14.99 price?

    _____

3. What would be the cost range, if Consolidated applied a markup of 25% of selling price and continued to aim for a $24.99 price?

    _____

4. Due to depressed textile markets, the manufacturer was able to obtain a particularly attractive price on a premium cotton fabric. His cost for UGLI JAMS using this fabric would normally have been $18.42. What would these have sold for at retail applying his, and Consolidated's normal pricing procedures?

    _____

5. What does your text call this approach to pricing?

    _____

21 Chain Discounts

Select Marketing Arithmetic, Chain Discounts, then Channel Discounts from *The MART's* menus. Use this model to complete the following exercises. Markup refers to markup on selling price, unless otherwise indicated.

Section_____   Name_____

                                                     Student Number_____

Assignment

1.   Gusto Cola sells for $1.00 a bottle at retail. Markups are 50% at retail and 25% at
     wholesale. The manufacturer's markup is 30%. What is the manufacturer's cost?

     _____

2.   Twin Creeks Candy Wholesalers purchases Mercury bars for $.50. It adds a margin of
     15% and the retailer's margin is 25%. What does a Mercury bar sell for at retail?

     _____

     What is the manufacturer's cost, if the markup at that level is 20%?

     _____

3.   Uncle Bart's Bakery produces a single product: Kuppies, a premium cream filled
     chocolate cupcake. Retailers sell them for $2.00 a pack and receive a 70% markup.
     They are stocked three times a week by a truck wholesaler whose markup is 45%.

     What does the retailer pay for a pack of Kuppies?

     _____ __

     What is Bart's price to the wholesaler?

     _____

     What is Bart's cost if the markup is 35%?

     _____

4. Fill in the missing entries in the tables.

	Retailer		Wholesaler		Producer	
	$	%	$	%	$	%
Selling Price						
Markup		50				54
Cost	777		234			

	Retailer		Wholesaler		Producer	
	$	%	$	%	$	%
Selling Price	892		435			
Markup						
Cost			211		150	

	Retailer		Wholesaler		Producer	
	$	%	$	%	$	%
Selling Price					333	
Markup		44		44		
Cost					191	

22 Bernais Specialty Foods

More Complex Discount Problems

It's Sunday afternoon and Straun Bernais, owner of Bernais Specialty Foods, a retailer, is catching up on paying his bills. The first invoice is for extracts having a retail value of $75.40. It indicates that wholesalers are allowed a 17% discount and retailers 28%. He is entitled to a stocking allowance of 3.75% for carrying a full assortment and a 10% discount for having placed his order during a manufacturer's promotion. He is working on Sunday to get these payments in the mail in order to earn the cash discounts. The terms are 2/10 net 30.

Assignment

Select Marketing Arithmetic, then Chain Discounts, then Many Discounts from *The MART's* menus. Use this model to complete the following exercises.

1.   What is the amount of the payment due?

_____

The second is for an assortment of candied fruit which he will sell for $300.   Retailers are allowed a 32% discount and wholesalers 19%. He has placed a newspaper ad which entitles him to an advertising allowance of 5%. He placed his order before October 1, which earned him a seasonal discount of 7%. The terms are 4/10 net 90.

2.   What amount is due?

_____

The third is for a shipment of 42 cases of Gourmet Dog Food (24 cans each). The discount for retailers is 20% and for wholesalers 14%. It is a new product and the manufacturer allowed an additional 3% to retailers during the introductory period. An order of this size entitles Straun to a quantity discount of 2%. Ordering a wide flavor assortment is worth another 1.5% stocking allowance. The product will sell for $2.00 a can ($2,106) and is subject to a sales tax collected at retail of 8%. Terms are 2/10 net 30.

3.   What amount is due?

_____

The last item is an electric bill for $297.66 which must arrive at the utility's business office tomorrow in order to earn the cash discount. Terms are 1/10 net 20. Straun can get it there on time only by sending it by messenger for a fee of $15.

4.   What should Straun do about the electric bill?

_____

BERNAIS SPECIALTY FOODS

Overheard in a restaurant at lunch. "I can get three tens and two fives from your competition on those 90 degree els." "OK. I'll let you have them for three tens, two fives and a ten." What's happening here?

In industries where pricing is extremely flexible, price lists would be out of date before they were printed. In such instances, one frequently finds relatively unchanging list prices with individual sales negotiated as adjustments to those prices. In the example, the first speaker claims to have been offered five separate discounts (three of 10% and two of 5%), applied as a discount chain, from the prevailing list price. The second speaker has countered with an additional 10% discount. (A 90 degree el is a pipe fitting which makes a right angle turn.)

5.   Suppose the list price of 90 degree els is $1.79. What is the dollar amount of the first price?

_____

6.   How much lower is the second price?

_____

7.   How much difference would it have made if the second price had been four tens and two fives instead of three tens, two fives and a ten?

_____

23 Twigg's Auto Parts

Cash Discounts

Mason Twigg was sole proprietor of an automobile parts supply store. In a high school business course she had learned that you should always take a cash discount, no matter what. An article in a regional trade association newsletter had taken the position that this was not the case. Manufacturers and parts wholesalers were offering terms that didn't make early payment advisable.

Mason has a line of credit at the local bank at prime plus 2%. If she takes fewer cash discounts, the balance on the line of credit, and her interest costs, will decline. Her bank's prime rate is currently 12%.

Assignment

Select the Cash Discounts option from the Marketing Arithmetic menu and evaluate the following invoices to see if taking the discount is advisable. Record your results in the table provided.

Paint for store premises: Gross amount $350.00. No functional discount. Terms 2/10, net 30.

Stationery: Gross amount $39.99. No functional discount. Terms 3/30, net 120.

Replace broken display window: Gross amount $125.00. No functional discount. Terms 2/5, net 25.

Spark Plugs: Gross amount $2,000. Functional discount 25%. Terms 2.5/20, net 90.

Winter Snow Tires: Gross amount $4,987.50. Functional discount 30%. Terms 4/10, net 180.

Air filters: Gross amount $398.66. Functional discount 33%. Terms 0.5/10, net 20.

Windshield Washer Fluid: Gross amount $249.90. Functional discount 17%. Terms 1.5/15, net 45.

Assorted GM parts: Gross amount $750.39. Functional discount 40%. Terms 1/10, net 20.

Rebuilt Jeep engine: Gross amount $1,050. Functional discount 25%. Terms 2/15, net 60.

Invoice	Amount After		Equivalent Annual Percentage Rate	Take Cash Discount?
	Functional Discount	Cash Discount		
Paint				
Stationery				
Window Replacement				
Spark Plugs				
Snow Tires				
Air Filters				
Washer Fluid				
GM Parts				
Jeep Engines				

The paint and window replacement have what appear to be very different terms, yet the equivalent annual percentage rate is the same. Why is that?

_____

_____

_____

_____

24 Williams' Notions: Markdowns

It is Sunday December 26. Jay Williams is preparing his shop for Monday's opening. He has advertised a sale on holiday merchandise and is in the process of repricing his stock. Give Jay a hand by determining the values of the missing entries in the following table.

Assignment

Use the Marketing Arithmetic Markdown Model to complete this exercise.

Item	Original Price	Markdown $	New Price	Markdown % On	
				Original Price	New Price
Cards	$1.25			40.0%	
Toy Pistols	$4.99	$2.00			
Bows	$1.19		$.89		
Ribbons	$1.09			30.0%	
Dolls	$49.99				150.0%
Softballs	$3.99	$.50			
Teddy Bears	$29.98		$19.99		
Tinsel	$1.29			62.0%	
Tree Stands	$9.98		$2.99		
Gift Wrap	$1.39	$.70			

Jay is dismayed when he totals up the amount of the markdowns he will be taking.

1.   What factors should he consider in deciding whether or not to reduce an item's price?

_____

_____

_____

2.   Which of these factors do you feel to be most important?

_____

25 Wharfside Seafood: Markdowns

Wharfside Seafood's name is all the description needed. It's located beside the wharf near Harborton's Old Town development and it sells seafood, and only seafood. Ed Halburton, its owner, runs a real low overhead operation. Though he's moved into a building, he operates much as he did when he sold from a pushcart. He buys fish and shellfish from the wholesalers and brokers in the early morning six days a week, keeps it fresh on crushed ice and sells the lot before going home around dinner time.

Wharfside isn't open on Sunday because Harborton's Sunday Closing Law, unlike most Blue Laws, has never been tested in court. So far, no one has been interested in trying.

It's late in the afternoon on the Saturday before Labor Day. Ed bought more than usual this morning in anticipation of holiday crowds visiting Old Town's shops and museums. The traffic was there. Unfortunately, it seems they have red meat in mind for their holiday barbecue. Faced with the unpleasant prospect of being stuck with a load of rotting fish over a long weekend, Ed has decided markdowns are in order.

Assignment

Complete the following table for Ed using the Marketing Arithmetic Markdown model.

Item	Original Price	Markdown $	New Price	Markdown % On Original Price	Markdown % On New Price
Oysters	$3.49	$1.00			
Halibut	$7.99			40.0%	
Haddock	$4.99				150.0%
Cod	$2.99		$1.94		
Shrimp	$9.99			20.0%	
Clams	$1.69	$1.00			
Mussels		$.60	$.39		
Lobster	$6.99				40.1%
Tile Fish	$5.49			30.0%	
Squid Tubes	$2.99		$1.99		

1.   What factors should Ed consider in deciding whether to take these, or any markdowns?

_____

_____

_____

_____

2.   Are the dominant factors in Ed's decision different from those in the William's Notions case (p. 131) ?

_____

_____

_____

VII Product

26 Product Evaluation Checklists

Marketers at all levels are faced with the task of evaluating and comparing product proposals. As part of the new product development process, manufacturers need to weed out the losers and identify the potential winners as early as possible. Investment in a new product idea grows exponentially as it progresses towards full scale introduction.

Merchants' buyers and buying committees are swamped with potential additions to their lines proposed by enthusiastic salespersons. Shelf space and inventory dollars are limited. All proposals are not created equal. Some method of evaluating and selecting from among competing products is needed.

Product checklists and rating forms are frequently used to accomplish this task. The general form is that of the weighted linear compensatory model discussed in the section on attitudes. A set of dimensions considered important to the organization and relevant to the products likely to be evaluated is identified and rated as to importance. These dimensions vary widely in different applications. A soft drink bottler considering new flavors would likely use a very product specific set. A retailer considering the same soft drink flavors, along with proposals for a new frozen dessert and a reformulated headache remedy would use a much more general set.

Having settled on a set of dimensions and assigned them a value for relative importance to the organization, the competing proposals are then scored on the dimensions. The importance ratings are multiplied by the scores. The sum of these products is the overall score for an alternative. Such rating scales are illustrated in the following cases.

The checklist approach has several advantages. First, the process of generating and assigning importance ratings to the dimensions is useful, in and of itself. Second, it insures that all dimensions are considered for all proposals. Third, it builds some objectivity into the product selection process. Finally, the rating forms are useful devices for communicating product evaluations in complex organizations.

We have discussed the checklist approach as a method of comparing competing alternatives at a point in time. With experience, an organization may develop norms which any proposal must meet to be worthy of consideration. If experience indicates that a product must score, say seven out of ten to be successful, then seven would become the cutoff for further consideration.

27 General Meadows' General Store

As a youth General Meadows cursed his parents for giving him the first name of General. However, during his time as a junior officer, calling an office and announcing that "this is Lieutenant General Meadows and I would like … " had been a source of no little amusement. When he had started his supermarket in Ashville, he couldn't resist the temptation to have a little more fun with his name.

The *Un* General Store

Meadows' store isn't a General Store in the old fashioned sense of carrying a range of merchandise which met most of a family's needs. Before opening the store, General noted reports that time constrained, two wage earner households were much less willing to shop for many types of products, such as children's everyday clothing and men's underwear, than in earlier years. Many shopping goods were coming to be viewed as convenience goods.

The General Store occupies about the floor space of an average supermarket. Part of the floor space is given over to an assortment of nonfashion clothing, so the assortment of food items offers less choice than a normal supermarket. Maximum use is made of vertical display of the soft goods to allow as much merchandise as possible to be shown without creating a cluttered appearance.

New Product Proposals

General is considering four new products or product lines for which he has received sales presentation in the last week. In a larger organization this decision would have been made by a buying committee. In this case it was a committee of one.

Silk Scarves. The first proposal is a line of silk scarves. They are relatively expensive and would be a departure from the nonfashion clothing that he has stocked to date. They carry a nice margin and General feels that, if properly displayed they could generate some impulse purchases. Also, a woman who wouldn't normally be caught dead buying clothing at the General Store might buy a fashionable scarf and a coordinated blouse.

Wine Kits. The second proposal is for the General Store to stock a line of home wine making supplies. It would handle a narrow range of grape juice concentrates and other items consumed in this hobby. Meadows would not sell equipment or attempt to compete with the wide product assortment offered by the specialty stores. According to the saleswoman, he could turn a nice profit by stocking about three reds and three whites. This would appeal to those hobbyists who would rather accept a restricted choice and make their purchase while doing routine shopping, than make a trip to the Grapevine on the other side of town.

Frozen Dessert. The third product was a new frozen dessert from a major food processor. The product had done well in test market and was being rolled out nationally with unusually heavy advertising. The General Store had limited freezer space and stocking this item would require dropping another item from the offering. General had given the samples left by the salesman to store employees to take home and try. Most were enthusiastic. One complained that the directions were unclear and she had burned the dessert. Though she was very efficient at her register, fellow employees said she couldn't follow the directions for instant coffee.

Vinegars. The final proposal under consideration was a line of flavored vinegars from a local entrepreneur. Gourmet cuisine had been the rage in the early to mid eighties and then interest had declined in favor of "down home cooking," at least in Ashland. General thought the pendulum was about ready to swing back in the other direction. He was somewhat concerned about the seller's ability to handle large volumes if the product really caught on.

Rating Device

Since he handled the buying task alone, Meadows worried about letting his personal reaction to a product or salesperson overly color a rational assessment of its prospects. To guard against this possibility, he had adapted a product rating form he had seen in a trade association newsletter, "Merchandising News and Views," to his needs. The original rating form had included a greater number of dimensions and had been set up so that each product was rated on a separate form. General had chosen those dimensions he felt were important and revised it so that ratings for several products were recorded on a single sheet. He then used a spreadsheet on his PC to perform the calculations.

This rating device is in Table 11. The user first assigns weights to the dimensions according to their importance to the enterprise. The weights are decimal fractions and must total to 1.0. It is important that the weights be assigned independently of the product, or product category being rated, if the form is to be used to compare different sorts of products.

Next, each product or proposal is rated on each of the dimensions. General used a five point scale, where 5 was the best rating. Having assigned ratings, each is multiplied by the corresponding importance weight. Finally, these products are summed to arrive at an overall score for each of the items under consideration.

Table 11 General Meadows' Product Rating Form

Rating Scale

5 - Very Good
4 - Good
3 - Average
2 - Poor
1 - Very Poor

	Weight	Item Rating			
		Silk Scarves	Wine Kits	Frozen Dessert	Gourmet Vinegar
Product appeal	.15	1	5	4	3
Does not duplicate existing item	.08	4	4	4	1
Margin/Profitability	.24	4	1	3	5
Advertising support	.02	4	5	4	3
Packaging	.05	4	2	3	3
Supplier	.12	1	5	2	4
Allowances and deals	.02	3	5	1	4
Shelf space required	.20	3	3	4	2
Test market results	.12	1	3	3	3
	1.00				

These sums can be used to compare any set of competing alternatives. With experience, one can develop norms or cutoff points which any individual product must meet before being selected as part of a store's offering.

Assignment

Select the Spreadsheet model from *The MART's* menu. Use this program to assist in completing the following exercises. If you have not read the description of the Spreadsheet model, you should do so now (p. 15).

1. This sort of approach to product screening is very common in larger retailing organizations. What purposes does it serve?

    _____

    _____

    _____

2. Do you feel this sort of a rating device is warranted in an organization where buying is a one person operation? Why or why not?

    _____

    _____

    _____

3. Why isn't margin/profitability alone a sufficient criterion for either a large or a small organization?

    _____

    _____

    _____

4. If General were to choose only one of the proposals, which would he choose?

    _____

    _____

5. Which proposal(s) would be selected if General followed a policy of accepting all proposals with a score of 3.0 or above?

_____

_____

_____

6. Which proposal would be chosen if the importance rating of margin/profitability were raised to 0.5?

_____

_____

_____

28 Reichman's Drugs

It was Sunday and Sunday was Bill Reichman's thinking day. This afternoon Bill was thinking about several new products that sales representatives had pitched to him in the preceding week. Two assistant managers shared the task of routine reordering to replenish merchandise stocks. Deciding on which new products to accept was a task Reichman reserved to himself.

Store History

Reichman Drugs was founded around the turn of the century and had been in Bill's family ever since. It was a single unit enterprise and was not associated with any of the chains. (Like many independent merchants, Bill's family had never had aspirations for growth in retailing and had invested profits from the store in other opportunities.)

The store was in what had been a middle class neighborhood of Victorian homes. It had undergone a period of decline from the mid fifties until around 1980 and the store found itself serving an aging population. This wasn't all bad, particularly for its prescription drug business. Gentrification had set in during the early eighties and Bill found affluent baby boomers constituted an increasing proportion of his traffic.

Positioning

Reichman's positioned itself as a family drug store and was something of a neighborhood institution. Bill took pride in knowing most of his customers by name and encouraged the pharmacists and clerks to at least note and use the names on prescriptions and credit cards.

The store's specialty was service. The pharmacy was intentionally overstaffed to minimize waiting for prescriptions to be filled. It had been the first independent in the city to computerize records so as to provide customers with information needed for their tax returns. Telephone orders for refills were actively encouraged. Bill or one of his assistants would make a delivery, on occasion, if a customer could not get out to pick up a prescription.

New Products

Bill was considering three new products, or product lines.

Seductively Yours Cosmetics. The first product under consideration was a new line of cosmetics offered by a British manufacturer. The line was more expensive than those normally carried by drug stores and promised a higher margin. It had been overwhelmingly successful in Britain, largely, it is believed, due to very explicit TV advertisements. Bill questioned whether the advertising themes would work as well when executed for the more restrictive codes governing advertising in the US.

Electronic Blood Pressure Monitor. This device was manufactured by a leading Japanese electronics firm. It was extremely simple to use and gave readings of blood pressure and pulse in under 40 seconds. Those who had been diagnosed as having high blood pressure and those in racial/ethnic groups who were at unusual risk were the obvious customers. However, according to the sales representative, they sold well to the fitness crowd and others concerned with health. They were particularly popular as gifts for "the athlete who has everything." The price of $99.99 seemed pretty stiff when one considered that Reichman's currently carried a manual blood pressure kit retailing for $29.99 and that it cost nothing to take one's pulse.

Private Label Merchandise. Since it wasn't affiliated with any sort of chain, Reichman's had carried only national brands. A local businessman had approached Bill with an innovative idea. He had obtained some packaging equipment and a printing facility which employed desktop publishing type technology. His business consisted of buying products like aspirin in bulk, packaging them in retail quantities and putting an individual store's label on the bottle. He could make these products available at prices slightly above those paid by the chains for private label merchandise, but substantially below those of national brands. He wanted Bill to give the idea a try by taking a shipment of "Reichman's Aspirin." It would be priced below the national brands, but yield a higher margin.

Bill found this idea attractive as his sales of non-prescription drugs were below most stores of comparable size. He suspected that many of his customers stocked up on these items at the discounters, rather than pay his prices for advertised brands.

Evaluating Alternatives

Reichman had obtained a copy of the new product rating form used by the buying committee of a regional drug chain and adapted it to his needs. The original version had included a larger number of dimensions and had been set up so that each product was rated on a separate form. Bill had chosen those dimensions he felt were important and revised it so that ratings for several products were recorded on a single sheet. He then used a spreadsheet on his PC to perform the calculations.

This rating device is shown in Table 12. The user first assigns weights to the dimensions according to their importance to his or her enterprise. The weights are decimal fractions and must total to 1.0. It is important that the weights be assigned independently of the product or product category being rated, if the form is to be used to compare different sorts of products.

Table 12 Reichman's Drugs product rating form

Rating Scale

5 – Very Good
4 – Good
3 – Average
2 – Poor
1 – Very Poor

	Weight	Item Rating		
		Seductively Yours Cosmetics	Blood Pressure Monitor	Private Label Aspirin
Product appeal	.16	1	2	4
Does not duplicate existing item	.12	3	5	4
Margin/Profitability	.18	1	4	4
Advertising support	.14	2	5	4
Packaging	.02	3	2	5
Supplier	.14	5	3	2
Allowances and deals	.02	2	3	3
Shelf space required	.07	4	4	3
Test market results	.15	5	2	1
	1.00			

Next, each product or proposal is rated on each of the dimensions. Bill used a five point scale, where 5 was the best rating. Having assigned ratings, each is multiplied by the corresponding importance weight. Finally, these products are summed to arrive at an overall score for each of the products under consideration.

These sums can be used to compare any set of competing alternatives. With experience, one can develop norms or cutoff points which any individual product must meet before being selected as part of a store's offering.

Assignment

Select Spreadsheet from *The MART's* menu. Use this program to assist in completing the following exercises.

1. This sort of approach to product screening is very common in larger retailing organizations. What purposes does it serve?

    _____

    _____

    _____

2. Do you feel this sort of a rating device is warranted in an organization where buying is a one person operation? Why or why not?

    _____

    _____

    _____

3. Why isn't margin/profitability alone a sufficient criterion for either a large or a small organization?

    _____

    _____

    _____

4.   If Reichman were to choose only one of the proposals, which would he choose?

_____

_____

_____

5.   Which proposal(s) would be selected if General followed a policy of accepting all proposals with a score of 3.0 or above?

_____

_____

_____

6.   Which proposal would be chosen if the importance rating of product appeal were raised to 0.4?

_____

_____

_____

29 Brand Positioning

How does the consumer view our brand? What do they think of us? What should we change in order to attract more customers? Is there room in the market for a new brand? When marketers want to know where they stand in the eyes of the consumer, these are the types of questions they ask. The novice will assume they can go out and ask the consumer what they think about the brand.

This only elicits vague comments such as "I like it.", "It tastes good.", "It doesn't work.", "It's too expensive." These types of comments are of little value, since they don't tell you whether these factors are important in the purchase of the product, how your brand fares compared to competing brands, and what changes might be necessary to influence the consumer's brand choice.

Marketers need to know where they stand on factors that are important in influencing the consumer's brand choice. As well as knowing where they stand, they have to know how to change and how these changes can be expected to impact on their sales or market share. This type of analysis is referred to as product positioning. Al Ries and Jack Trout, in their landmark book entitled *Positioning: The Battle For Your Mind*, defined positioning in the following manner.[1]

Positioning starts with a product. A piece of merchandise, a service, a company, an institution, or even a person ... But positioning is not what you do to a product. Positioning is what you do to the mind of the prospect. That is, you position the product in the mind of the prospect.

Notice that the term product can refer to more than a physical product. Included would be such things as services and stores.

There are many consumer models that can be used to help the marketer develop a positioning strategy. We will focus on one model that has the components that make the most intuitive sense when positioning a brand.

---

[1]Al Ries and Jack Trout, *Positioning: The Battle for Your Mind* (New York: Warner Books, 1982).

The Model

Here is the model.

$$A_a = \Sigma_{i=1}^{n} \; w_i \; * \; (c - |b_{ia} - IP_i|)$$

The model describes a person's attitude, A_a, toward some act, such as purchasing a particular brand, or shopping at a particular store. It is assumed that a person will more likely purchase that particular brand or shop at that particular store, the more positive the attitude.

The right side of the equation takes into account the evaluative criteria that people use to judge the brands. For toothpaste we might find that brand choice is based on whether purchasing the brand will lead to whiter teeth, less tooth decay, strong, healthy gums, and a pleasant taste in the mouth when brushing.

For each criterion we need to know three things:

Beliefs/perceptions on each criterion for each act, b_{ia}. How do consumers actually rate the purchase of various brands on the evaluative criteria? How would they perceive the purchase of a particular brand of toothpaste leading to whiter teeth, decay prevention, strong gums and a pleasant taste? When we determine the position of the brand it is based on perceptions such as these, and it is these perceptions that must be changed in order to reposition the product in the consumer's mind.

Importance weight for that criterion, w_i. Knowing where you are positioned on a particular criterion does not tell you whether it is worthwhile to change people's perceptions on that dimension. You first want to find out whether that dimension is an important factor in brand selection. For example, everybody may rate your brand as superior in taste compared to all of your competitors, but if taste is not an important criterion for brand selection, then this favorable position probably has little influence on market share.

Ideal Point for that criterion, IP_i. On some dimensions, consumers may want to purchase a brand positioned somewhere in the middle of the dimension, rather than at the extremes. Also, some consumers may differ significantly in what they want from a product. Even for price we do not always want to buy the least expensive product. For toothpaste we may want some mint flavor, others may not. At a store or restaurant one individual may want some service, but not too much; others may want more or less service.

In order to know what direction to change perceptions and by how much, we need to know the ideal point on each dimension. Many models leave this element out and assume the evaluative criteria can be defined in such a way that one extreme or the other is superior for all people. However, they are not as useful for positioning as an ideal point model.

The other variable, *c*, is a constant which is included for convenience so that less discrepancy between the ideal point and the person's actual belief results in a higher rating. It is assumed the consumer will purchase the brand with the highest attitude score, all else being equal.

The beliefs, ideal points, and importance weights are all measured on a six point scale and the constant is 6. If the belief and ideal point are the same on a particular criterion (e.g. each is 5 on the 6 point scale) then the |Belief-Ideal Point| term will equal 0. When this is subtracted from the constant 6 we are left with a perception rating of 6. A high perception rating multiplied by a high importance weight would add as much as 36 to the attitude score. If on the other hand the belief and the ideal point are at opposite extremes of the scale (e.g. a 6 and a 1) the difference of 5 will be subtracted from the constant 6 leading to a value of 1 for the perception rating. This value, when multiplied by the importance weight will add only a 6 to the attitude score.

When considering where to reposition their brand, or whether to introduce a new one, the marketer would like to keep these three components — belief, ideal point and importance — in mind. Also, if there are several important criteria then a change in perception on one criterion may have little impact on the overall attitude, and therefore on brand choice. The impact of any changes on one dimension should be evaluated in the context of all the dimensions.

If there are four brands, stores or other alternatives, four attitude scores will be generated using the formula. The assumption is that a person will select the brand or store with the highest score. This assumption may not be totally accurate for any one individual, but it has been found to be reasonable over large samples of consumers.

The Program

There are two product positioning cases. The first is a relatively uncomplicated product positioning case called Flash Toothpaste. The second, Wilson's Shoes, is a more complex case dealing with store image.

Once you have selected a case you will be presented with six bar graphs on the screen. The four graphs on the left present the distribution of beliefs for the four brands/stores on the criterion noted at the top of the screen. The graph in the upper right hand corner of the screen presents the distribution of the ideal points on this same criterion. The lower right corner graph presents the distribution of the importance weights on this criterion.

These graphs can be examined to help decide which set of beliefs could be changed to increase market share. Changing perceptions would probably be profitable where the bulk of consumers rate your brand differently from the ideal points on evaluative criteria rated as important.

To examine another set of beliefs, ideal points and importance weights for another criterion, use the left or right arrow keys. Once you have reviewed the graphs for the four evaluative criteria hit page down <Pg Dn> and select pairs of dimensions to graph.

Positioning Map

These graphs present the position of the brands, represented by their mean values, on each dimension (these positions are often referred to as centroids). Also printed on the graph are the numbers of respondents that selected particular ideal points. To the right of the graph is the estimated market share based on the model. These market share figures may have little in common with the actual market shares, since many factors not included in the model can influence brand or store choice. However, all else equal, an improvement in market share here should indicate a chance for an improvement in the firm's real market share.

Normally, one would examine these graphs and decide, based on the distance and direction of the ideal points from the brand's centroid, and the relative location of the competitors, which perceptions to change and in what direction. You can, however, move the centroid for your brand around the graph using the arrow keys and then hit enter to recalculate your market share. The computer adjusts each respondent's belief rating on a dimension so that the mean for all respondents corresponds to the new mean you have selected (by positioning the cursor) on the screen. New attitude scores are calculated for each respondent and the resulting market shares are reported.

Keep in mind that it may be easy to move the centroid to a new location on the graph, but impossible to shift actual consumer perceptions that far. It's up to you to decide what would be a reasonable distance to shift perceptions. Sometimes it will be necessary to recommend the introduction of a new brand or a new store, rather than trying to reposition an existing brand or store.

30 Flash Toothpaste

Glenn, the product manager of Flash toothpaste has just completed collecting data which will help him decide which of four campaigns would be most appropriate for his brand. The four options are: a) to continué to emphasize the ability of Flash to *whiten teeth,* b) to emphasize Flash's ability to *prevent tooth decay,* c) to strengthen the toothpaste's *minty flavor* and appeal to those looking for a strong mint flavored toothpaste, or d) to add new ingredients to the product which will *strengthen* people's *gums,* thus reducing the chances of gum disease. He feels these four criteria are the most important in brand selection.

Competitive Environment

Flash has three main competitors, Chomper's, Fang and Roots. Flash's market share has declined to 12%, with its major competitors, Chomper's and Fang gaining at Flash's expense. People's perceptions of these three brands and Flash, along with the importance weights and ideal points on the evaluative criteria, are available in the product positioning program. High ratings are associated with an ability to whiten teeth, prevent tooth decay, strengthen gums and with a minty taste. A 6 on the importance scale indicates the criterion is very important, while a 1 indicates it is very unimportant.

Assignment

1. What are the strengths and weaknesses of each brand? Do they have a unique selling proposition?

    Flash:

    _____

    _____

    _____

    Chomper's:

    _____

    _____

    _____

    Fang:

    _____

    _____

    _____

    Roots:

    _____

    _____

    _____

2. Examine the distribution of perceptions, ideal points and importance weights for each of the evaluative criteria. Is there any opportunity for improving Flash's position on any of the dimensions? Why or why not?

Prevents cavities:

_____

_____

_____

Whitens teeth:

_____

_____

_____

Minty flavor:

_____

_____

_____

Strengthens gums:

_____

_____

_____

Section_____ Name_____

Student Number_____

3. Consumers can be grouped into benefit segments where the members of each segment tend to place importance on particular dimensions. One benefit segment might feel that decay prevention is most important while others may not. Is there evidence of distinct benefit segments in the distribution of importance weights? What benefit segments appear to exist?

_____

_____

_____

_____

4. Select two criteria and an improved market position for Flash toothpaste and fill out the table below. Keep in mind that movement of more than 1 – 2 points may be quite costly.

Name of first criterion   _____

Name of second criterion   _____

	Original Position	New Position
Position on first criterion	_____	_____
Position on second criterion	_____	_____
Market share of: Flash	_____	_____
Chomper's	_____	_____
Fang	_____	_____
Roots	_____	_____

FLASH TOOTHPASTE

5.   Which campaign should Glenn use? With which brands will he be competing? Which
      brands would lose market share to Flash?

_____

_____

_____

_____

31 Wilson's Shoes

Wilson's Shoes is an independently owned shoe store in downtown Wolfburg. The store is located in one of the city's primary, upscale shopping areas. With 40 feet of window display frontage, the store attracts many of its shoppers off the street. Seven years ago the new owner, Mr. Clarkson, decided to specialize in women's shoes by offering a very wide selection of sizes and styles, particularly suitable for the older woman who needs the variety of sizes and is more interested in comfort than fashion. This strategy worked very well, but Mr. Clarkson now wishes to expand his market by shifting his market position.

Market Segments

Previous research found three main segments, each making up about a third of the market. First, there are those people who make up the bulk of his present customers. These people, called the *Comfort Seekers*, are mainly interested in a wide selection of comfortable, moderately stylish shoes. They are willing to spend extra to obtain the size and comfort they seek.

Those in the second segment are called the *Fashion Seekers*. They tend to be younger women working in an office environment. They are very concerned with fashion, not particularly price sensitive, and not as concerned with assortment and service.

Those in the third segment are called the *Value Seekers*. They are not as concerned with fashion or selection, and only slightly more concerned with service. They are, however, quite concerned about price.

Competitors

Wilson's has three main competitors in its immediate trading area. These are:

Nature: This store, located in a nearby mall, features casual and fashionable shoes, and tends to advertise their wide selection and quality service.

European Shoes: This store is situated across the street from Wilson's and stocks a wide range of highly fashionable shoes shipped in from Europe. As one woman put it, "One look at the window display and you know you'll have to pay a fortune for the shoes, but they'll be stylish."

Bell's: This store, located in the same nearby mall, is part of a large chain of department stores. Bell's store offers a fairly wide selection of medium priced shoes (which often are put on sale), but due to a high turnover of staff, the quality of service is relatively poor.

Data was collected in a telephone survey of 50 women. High ratings are associated with good service, a wide selection of brands and sizes, an assortment of stylish shoes and **higher** prices. A 6 on the importance scale indicates the criterion is very important while a 1 indicates it is very unimportant.

Assignment

1. Examine the graphs associated with each criterion. How much potential is there for gaining market share by changing perceptions in each case? Why?

Price:

_____

_____

_____

Service:

_____

_____

_____

Fashion:

_____

_____

_____

Selection:

_____

_____

_____

2. What is the maximum market share figure that can be obtained by moving Wilson's centroid to any position on any of the graphs?

Wilson's market share _____

First criterion _____ Perception rating _____

Second criterion _____ Perception rating _____

Who loses market share to Wilson's and why?

_____

_____

_____

_____

3. Assume Wilson's can only move one position in each direction from the original position. What is the highest attainable market share figure?

Wilson's market share _____

First criterion _____ Perception rating _____

Second criterion _____ Perception rating _____

Who loses market share to Wilson's and why?

_____

_____

_____

_____

4. According to the model, is it possible to compete with Bell's? How does understanding what segments exist in the market place help in this analysis?

_____

_____

_____

_____

5. Is it more advisable to go after Nature or Europe in order to gain market share? Why?

_____

_____

_____

_____

VIII Pricing

32 Marginal Analysis

As you may know from your previous courses, economic or marginal analysis is the theoretically correct solution to setting prices. Unlike other approaches to price setting, such as markup pricing and breakeven analysis, marginal analysis can help us determine the optimal, or profit maximizing price.

Admittedly, this approach is demanding when it comes to the data requirements. You might feel that if you knew that much about your market, you wouldn't have a pricing problem. Nevertheless, it is the authors' position that making best guesses at demand at different prices is superior to ignoring the task and hoping no one will notice.

All approaches to pricing involve some assumption, often hidden, about the level of demand. Take a simple markup (markon) rule such as "determine variable cost and add 100%." There's no demand estimate there, right? Wrong. The 100% being added is supposed to contribute to fixed costs and, it is hoped, leave something for profit. How much is contributed depends entirely upon the number of units sold: demand. The implicit demand assumption is that, at the markup chosen, enough items will be sold to make a satisfactory contribution.

The Marginal Analysis Program

When using the marginal analysis program, one may either enter values for a new problem, or analyze data stored for one of the cases below. To enter new data, you will need to know the minimum and maximum prices being considered and be able to estimate the quantity that will be sold at each. You will also need an initial estimate of fixed and variable costs.

Don't worry if you make a mistake when entering data. You will soon have a chance to make changes to anything but your chosen prices. (If the price range must be changed return to the marginal analysis menu when given the opportunity.) If you choose to analyze case data this information is already stored on the program disk.

After your entries are complete, the results of initial calculations will be displayed. The computer will have divided the difference between your lowest and highest prices into a number of equal intervals. Demand at each of these points is estimated, assuming a linear relationship.

Changing Values

Some values will be shown on a red background. Initially these are on the top and bottom lines. Information in red blocks is, temporarily, fixed; it can only be changed by moving the cursor to that location and entering a new value. Entering a value anywhere else in the table creates a new fixed point. Values between any two fixed points are automatically recalculated.

For fixed and variable costs, the new value will be used from the point at which an entry is made up to, but not including, the next fixed point. Changes in quantity are determined by interpolating between the point at which an entry is made and the nearest points above and below that are already fixed. An example will help clarify how this is done.

Suppose your initial screen included the following data.

	Price	Quantity	Total Fixed Cost	Average Variable Cost
top line	2.00	99,999	2,000	1.00
some middle line	4.11	95,526	2,000	1.00
bottom line	10.00	55,000	2,000	1.00

The top and bottom lines will be shown on a red background. If you were to change fixed cost on the bottom line to 3,000 or average variable cost to 1.10, the new values will be shown, and used in the calculations, for all lines up to the line below the top line; the line with the lowest price and highest quantity. If you were to move to a line in the middle of the screen and make the same entry, values below the entry point will remain unchanged. Values from the entry point to the line below the top will be changed to the new value. The point where the new entry was made becomes fixed and will be shown on red.

If you were to change the quantity on the top or bottom row, say the bottom row to 40,000, new quantity estimates will be made for all prices between $10.00 and $2.00. Were you, instead, to change the value in the middle (95,526), to a new value, say 80,000, you will have created two ranges (and a nonlinear demand curve). Above this point the program will estimate quantities by interpolating between 80,000 and 99,999. Below, it would interpolate between 55,000 and 80,000.

Any number of changes can be made. Since each creates a new fixed point, things can begin to get messy. If so, simply return to the menu and reload the data set.

Profit Screen. On the second (profit) screen total revenue, cost and profit will be displayed along with the marginal values. The values yielding the maximum profit of all the prices tested will be shown on magenta. You can only change quantities on this screen. Having made such a change, you will be returned to the first screen, so any other changes you wish to make can be entered.

You cannot change a price displayed on either of the screens. (Allowing price changes in earlier versions seemed to confuse users.) However, an equivalent change results if you change the quantity at any of the prices that are displayed.

Graphic Display

After viewing either tabular screen, you can choose to look at a graphic presentation of the results. In some instances these will be enlightening. In others they will look messy and confusing, particularly if there are changes in costs over the ranges being graphed or the range of values in a single graph is particularly large. That's what the world is like.

Zooming In

The program can be used like a zoom lens. Suppose you initially try a broad range of prices and find the maximum profit lies between prices of $100 and $200. Record the quantity estimates at these prices, the fixed costs and variable costs, then return to the marginal analysis menu. Select "Enter Problem Data." Enter $100 as the minimum price and $200 as the maximum, along with the appropriate quantities and costs. The program will then analyze prices in this interval.

Saving Work

You may save either new data, or interim results from analyzing a case to disk. Be sure to select a file name different from any file on the disk. Reusing a file name will result in the loss of the original file. The file saved will contain the results of any changes made since calling the case or entering new data.

33 Pamper Yourself

Pamper Yourself, Inc., manufactures high quality candies and confections. These are sold though candy wholesalers to specialty retailers, and the candy departments in upscale department stores. Pamper's major competition is from Swiss and German imports.

Pamper's channel members handled too many products for them to give much attention to pricing individual items. The manufacturer's suggested retail price was looked upon as if carved in stone. Dealers considered their traditional markups to be nonnegotiable.

Pricing was, thus, left almost entirely to the manufacturer. This did not mean that the candy makers thought they had much freedom in pricing. If channel members felt that a product, or a manufacturer's entire line was not moving because of its price, they would simply drop it, with little or no notice.

Pricing

Price setting at Pamper Yourself had simply evolved without much thought. Jan Withers had begun candy making as a hobby and found that she had a real talent for developing new flavor combinations and product variations. Jan had been more than happy to fill her friends orders at out-of-pocket cost, because that meant they were paying the price for her hobby. Her friends, who had frequently told her she should do it for a living, lost a good deal when she took their advice and began selling through local retailers. She still priced at ingredient cost plus something for her time and a bit of her mortgage.

When Jan's candies became an instant success, taking over an idle candy plant with the help of a silent partner followed naturally. Pamper Yourself, Inc., prospered and now served the Great Lakes region, New England and the Middle Atlantic seaboard from a gleaming new plant in eastern Pennsylvania. The silent partner had become active and handled financial functions. Jan supervised product development and production, herself. Clive Williams, the marketing manager, had recently been hired from a lingerie manufacturer.

Price setting hadn't evolved much beyond Jan's kitchen. Products were divided into six, relatively homogeneous, product lines. Each product line was assigned a share of the overhead and administrative costs and of a target profit. Using current variable cost and the sales volume of the same quarter from the prior year, a breakeven price was determined. This price, along with the traditional markups for the channel, determined the manufacturer's suggested retail price. As long as this price was below the price of comparable imports, it was accepted. Pamper Yourself's prices averaged 30% – 40% below those of its foreign competitors.

The Winds of Change

Two factors had caused Pamper Yourself's principals to rethink their pricing practices. The falling US dollar had made imports more expensive, while having a much smaller effect on Pamper Yourself's costs. This created some slack to the upside. The second factor was the arrival of Clive Williams. Clive argued that luxury products such as Pamper's weren't particularly price sensitive and that, in fact, a high price could even increase sales.

Clive had hired a market research firm to do focus group interviews with candy purchasers. Several themes emerged that deserved further study. Most important in the present context were "exceptional value" and "as good as any for much less." Clive thought that Pamper Yourself might, in fact, be offering "excessive value" at the expense of the bottom line.

A second study was commissioned to estimate the sensitivity of sales of quality candy to price. The results were used to predict sales of the 750 gram box of filled chocolates at prices over the relevant range. Clive has a commitment from Jan and her partner to allow him to use this information to set prices on this item for the next year.

Assignment

Select Pricing: Marginal Analysis from *The MART's* menu and complete the following exercises. The demand estimates developed from this study are stored on the program disk under the filename Pamper.dat, which you should enter when the program requests a filename.

1.   What price and quantity result in the greatest profit?

     Price

     _____

     Quantity

     _____

2.   The row highlighted in magenta simply produces the highest profit of any price tried. It may not be the profit maximizing price. To investigate this use the zoom feature.

     Record the values from the rows above and below the row highlighted.

Price	Quantity	Total Fixed Cost	Ave Variable Cost	Marginal Revenue	Marginal Cost
_____ above	_____	_____	_____	_____	_____
_____ below	_____	_____	_____	_____	_____

Press <Esc> to go to the menu and select "Enter User Data." Follow the prompts, entering the values you recorded above. Where is the greatest profit in this reduced range?

Price	Quantity	Total Fixed Cost	Ave Variable Cost	Marginal Revenue	Marginal Cost
_____ above	_____	_____	_____	_____	_____
_____ below	_____	_____	_____	_____	_____

Repeat the preceding step if you have not found the absolute maximum profit and your price increments are greater than a few cents.

Price	Quantity	Total Fixed Cost	Ave Variable Cost	Marginal Revenue	Marginal Cost
_____ above	_____	_____	_____	_____	_____
_____ below	_____	_____	_____	_____	_____

Repeat the preceding step if you have not found the absolute maximum profit and your price increments are greater than a few cents.

Price	Quantity	Total Fixed Cost	Ave Variable Cost	Marginal Revenue	Marginal Cost
_____ above	_____	_____	_____	_____	_____
_____ below	_____	_____	_____	_____	_____

3.   Does the range of prices examined in the study include the profit maximizing price?

_____

4.   What price would you recommend if fixed costs assigned to this product were doubled in order to reduce the fixed cost burden for another product?

_____

5.   Expectations of a poor harvest have driven up the prices of sugar which will increase variable costs by 20%. What does the profit maximizing price become?

_____

6.   Pamper Yourself uses a special chocolate in this product for which it contracts on an annual basis, based upon production forecasts. Producing over 60,000 boxes will strain supplier capacity which will push up the price. This will raise variable costs to $4.00. How does this affect the optimal price? (If over 60,000 units are produced, all output will be at the higher cost.)

_____

_____

34 Cosmic Clones

Cosmic Clones operated in the low tech end of the high tech business. The firm assembled PC compatible computers from readily available components bought from electronic wholesalers and brokers.

The firm was founded by Mark Jefferson in 1984. Jefferson had been employed as a salesman for a major name brand of computers, serving mostly educational and governmental organizations. As his customers became more sophisticated, Mark found the brand logo on his products offered less and less of an advantage. Even his major customers were experimenting with clones. He moaned, "People are buying computers like canned corn."

Jefferson leaned on some of his contacts for information. Components were in plentiful supply and markups on clones were comfortable. He became convinced that there was a major profit opportunity for anyone who could assemble and market compatibles, while controlling fixed costs. Cosmic Clones was born.

A Low Budget Operation

Jefferson did control fixed costs. He was the entire sales force as well as the delivery person and half of the manufacturing labor force. The machines were assembled on a plywood sheet in Jefferson's wooden garage on the outskirts of Warrenton. Utilities consisted of coal for the stove and electricity for a few overhead lights. Component inventory was kept to an absolute minimum and there was virtually no finished goods inventory, as the machines were made to order. Most customers couldn't wait to get their hands on their new toys, so they were picked up at nearly the instant they were finished.

Initially, the one man nature of Mark's operation impeded sales. Potential customers, even if they had complete faith in Mark and his machines, were concerned about future service. "I'd only be a heartbeat away from being left flapping in the wind."

Two factors relieved this fear. First, Mark entered into an agreement with a full service computer retailer in Warrenton. For a fixed fee per machine, the retailer agreed to honor Mark's service guarantee, if Mark's business or Mark should cease to exist. The retailer backed this assurance with a performance bond.

The other factor was a fortuitous sale. Mark sold 50 machines to the city university's School of Business, which had previously purchased only IBM brand machines. People, particularly faculty, felt that if the school had that large an investment in Cosmic machines, it would have to find a source of service, even if Mark and the retailer and the bonding agency all turned belly up. Someone would be found to service the machines, even if some cost were involved.

The university's purchase also tended to legitimize Mark's offering. Since the school had a major investment in PC software, fears as to the degree of compatibility of Mark's machines were soothed.

Pricing in a Changing Environment

At the outset Mark had the market pretty much to himself. Assemblers of compatibles from outside the region did not enjoy his personal reputation, or the advantages of his perceived link with the University. Brand loyalists bought name brands and others bought Cosmics, for considerably less. Pricing was simple. When a prospective customer had specified a configuration, Mark estimated the price that would be charged for the same machine wearing a name brand and cut it by 30%. Take it or leave it. Mark likened it to "assembling money."

Times have changed. The obvious customers, such as university faculty, accountants and engineers have a machine on their desk at work, and one at home. The name brands have come down in price and people, having become more accustomed to computers, are less sensitive about buying a clone, wherever it is made. Two new local competitors have begun operations. Collectively, things are a lot tougher than they once were. Mark still enjoys a differential advantage arising from his long (for this business) history and favorable word of mouth. However, it is apparent that pricing has to be done with a much sharper pencil.

Problem Data

A national trade association did a study estimating the price elasticity of a typical product, a 640 K, dual disk drive machine with 14" color monitor. Mark hired a consultant to adapt the findings to the Warrenton market. The resulting demand estimates, along with information concerning Cosmic Clones' costs, are stored on the program disk.

Select Pricing: Marginal Analysis from *The MART's* menu and complete the following exercises. The demand estimates developed from this study are stored on the program disk under the filename Cosmic.dat, which you should enter when the program requests you to specify a file.

Assignment

All prices, revenues and costs in the Cosmic data file are in hundreds of dollars. Entries should be similarly scaled. To try a variable cost of $1,299 enter 12.99.

1.   What price and quantity result in the greatest profit?

     Price

     _____

     Quantity

     _____

2.   The row shown highlighted in magenta simply produces the highest profit of any price tried. It may not be the profit maximizing price. To investigate this use the zoom feature. Record the values from the rows above and below the row highlighted.

Price	Quantity	Total Fixed Cost	Ave Variable Cost	Marginal Revenue	Marginal Cost
_____	_____	_____	_____	_____	_____
above
_____	_____	_____	_____	_____	_____
below

Go to the menu and select "Enter User Data." Follow the prompts, entering the values you recorded above. Where is the greatest profit in this reduced range?

Price	Quantity	Total Fixed Cost	Ave Variable Cost	Marginal Revenue	Marginal Cost
_____	_____	_____	_____	_____	_____
above
_____	_____	_____	_____	_____	_____
below

Repeat the preceding step if you have not found the absolute maximum profit and your price increments are greater than one dollar.

	Price	Quantity	Total Fixed Cost	Ave Variable Cost	Marginal Revenue	Marginal Cost
above	_____	_____	_____	_____	_____	_____
below	_____	_____	_____	_____	_____	_____

Repeat the preceding step if you have not found the absolute maximum profit and your price increments are greater than one dollar.

	Price	Quantity	Total Fixed Cost	Ave Variable Cost	Marginal Revenue	Marginal Cost
above	_____	_____	_____	_____	_____	_____
below	_____	_____	_____	_____	_____	_____

3. Does the range of prices examined in the study include the profit maximizing price?

_____

4. What price would you recommend if fixed costs were to double?

_____

5. Import restrictions have driven up the prices of chips which will increase variable costs by 20%. What does the profit maximizing price become?

_____

6.   Cosmic Clones contracts for cabinets on an annual basis based upon production
      forecasts. Producing over 300 machines will strain supplier capacity which will push
      up the price. This will raise variable costs to $1550. How does this affect the optimal
      price? (If output is over 300 units all cabinets must be purchased at the higher price.)

      _____

      _____

35 Breakeven Analysis

"I may not be able to guess at demand, but I sure know what my costs are." "If I can cover my costs, I won't lose money, even if I don't make any." These and similar, practical sounding arguments are often raised in support of breakeven analysis and other cost based approaches to pricing.

Breakeven analysis is a tool for examining the implications of choosing a particular price, based upon the relationships between price (*P*), fixed costs (*FC*), variable costs (*VC*) and the breakeven point (*BEP*). Each unit actually sold at a price contributes an amount (*P - VC*) towards covering fixed costs, assuming price is greater than variable cost. The point at which fixed costs are exactly met is called the breakeven point (*FC* = Units * (*P - VC*). If more units are sold, then the contribution becomes profit. By rearranging terms we can solve for the number of units which must be sold to just break even.

$$BEP = \frac{FC}{(P - VC)}$$

Breakeven Analysis is effectively presented in graphic form. The horizontal axis shows

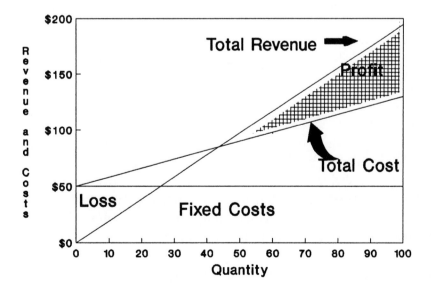

the quantity (Q) of units produced and sold; the vertical axis measures total revenue and total cost. The horizontal line is fixed costs, which do not vary as quantity changes. The upward sloping line rising from the intersection of FC and the vertical axis represent total costs (**FC + Q * VC**). Sales (**Q * P**) begin at the origin.

The area above and to the right of the intersection of total cost and total revenue curves represents profit. In the area below the BEP one would operate at a loss. (In the breakeven analysis program these areas are color coded, white for profit and magenta for loss.)

Unlike demand based approaches to price setting, such as marginal analysis, breakeven analysis, in and of itself, cannot identify a best — profit maximizing — price. However, coupled with managerial judgment, it can tell us some useful things about prices under consideration. All else being equal, low breakeven points are attractive. Of course, the units must, actually, be sold. Unrealistically high prices appear to produce low breakeven points.

The breakeven point can also be examined in the light of capacity limitations. If the units which must be sold to breakeven are beyond our capacity to produce, then we must reexamine the situation. Remember, we lose money on every unit sold before the breakeven point is reached. If reaching a sales level will require additional fixed costs or increase our variable costs, then we must redo the analysis using the higher costs.

Comparing the breakeven point to industry sales can be helpful. If industry sales are 200,000 and we arrive at a breakeven point of 100,000, that implies a 50% market share. Is that reasonable, given our knowledge of the market?

Have you noticed the weakness in the arguments given at the beginning of this section? Units must actually be sold. Market shares must be reasonable, etc. We can never avoid making estimates of demand. Yet, breakeven analysis can provide useful information.

Extensions

BEP – Dollars

Say you are trying to estimate the level of operations at which a supermarket will break even. It would seem that breakeven analysis would be of little use. Given the many thousands of individual items on the shelves, what is a unit? What is the price and variable cost of one unit? Or, say you're managing a small foundry producing cast metal objects ranging from high priced trophies to inexpensive novelties and, except for molds, all utilize the same basic plant and equipment. A similar problem.

As in many instances when we must add apples and oranges we use a common denominator, the dollar. Fixed costs are fixed costs in dollars, as before. Instead of contribution in dollars we divide both price and variable cost by price, yielding a divisor of contribution as a proportion of selling price.

$$BEP\text{-}\$ = \frac{FC}{(1.0 - VC)}$$

If fixed costs are \$800,000 and variable costs are 75% of sales (0.75 stated as a proportion), then the breakeven point is calculated as

$$BEP\text{-}\$ = \$3,200,000 = \frac{FC}{(1.0 - 0.75)}$$

Hint. Doesn't that look a lot like calculating BEP in units when the price of a unit is \$1.00 and the variable costs are \$0.75? Of course it does. It's exactly equivalent and the units under consideration are dollars.

Multiple Breakeven Analysis

As indicated above, we usually evaluate the results of breakeven analysis in the light of our implicit demand assumptions. It is often helpful to make these estimates explicit and to do

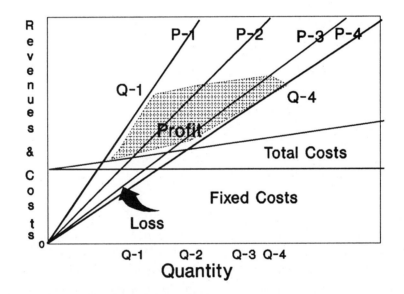

so for several prices over the relevant range. Admittedly, these are just best estimates of demand. However, they are an improvement over the implicit assumption of the preceding graph, that any quantity can be sold at the price under consideration. Assume that management is considering several prices in the relevant range. Further assume that management feels compelled to set prices at one of the prevailing price points of P-1, P-2, P-3, P-4. You, the analyst have talked to knowledgeable persons and arrived at the demand estimates Q-1, Q-2, Q-3, Q-4. The breakeven points and profits at the different price-quantity combinations are shown above.

Multiple breakeven analysis can, obviously, identify the most profitable of the prices being studied. It can also be of further help. In the example, the zone of profitability is relatively constant. If one has any confidence as to the quality of the demand estimates, a price could be selected with a reasonable degree of comfort. However if the profit zone were irregular, perhaps showing a pronounced peak at one price and a loss at one or more of the others, it would be well worthwhile to spend time and effort refining the demand estimates.

The Breakeven Analysis Program

The breakeven analysis program can handle all of the variations described above. The initial screen offers the user a choice between single and multiple breakeven analysis. If single breakeven analysis is chosen, you will be presented with a tabular screen in which the required values may be entered. Simply move the cursor and type in the desired values followed by < Enter >.

The program will perform its calculations as soon as it has sufficient data. If a unit price has been entered, or can be determined, the breakeven point in both units and dollars will be presented. If price is unknown, but a contribution margin can be determined, the breakeven point in dollars will be calculated.

After the solution is shown, you may make changes to any of the values entered or calculated by the program, and observe the impact on the solution. Whenever a solution is shown, you may opt to see a graphic display of the breakeven problem.

If multiple breakeven analysis is chosen from the initial menu, the program goes into graphics mode. You will be asked to enter values for fixed cost, variable cost and four prices with demand estimates at each. The program cannot proceed until four price-demand pairs have been entered. When all data has been provided, the solution will be shown in a graphical display. At least one price demand combination must be profitable for the solution to have any meaning. If this condition is not met an appropriate message will be displayed.

36 Vanity Front Page

Ruth Cunliffe helped support herself and her med student husband from the proceeds of Vanity Front Page. This was a little business producing novelty front pages of newspapers. By hooking a low priced laser printer to a personal computer, Vanity placed a customer's name in banner headlines and wherever a name would appear throughout the accompanying article. (*JEANIE WILSON MISS AMERICA; HOMEBOY, GRONSKY WINS GOLD*, etc.) The printer fed a full sheet of newspaper stock, which was preprinted except for the headline and the column containing the related article.

The preprinted page stock and disks with the articles to be customized were obtained from the company franchising the system. Ruth usually had about 15 alternatives on hand. The product sold for $2.50 a copy. She had paid cash for the equipment and the franchise fee and programs disks accounted for a major portion of the $1.25 a sheet she paid for the stock.

Ruth sold her "papers" at fairs, craft shows, neighborhood/ethnic festivals and anywhere else that it seemed people would purchase this sort of "just for fun" souvenir items. She liked her business because she could work when, where and as much as she wanted.

Ruth usually didn't schedule any shows over the Christmas break. However, this year she finished exams earlier than usual and her husband finished late, so she would have time on her hands. She was considering a flyer promoting space at the Kris Kringle show at the Westside Mall. A spot of the size she will need costs $500 for the Friday noon to Sunday night show. Promoters require that the space be "substantially occupied" during those hours. (It is customary to overlook absences to pick up a meal to take back to one's booth, or to use the facilities, as long as valuables are not left unattended.)

Ruth has never paid more than $200 for a spot for a similar length of time, so she is concerned. In addition, her one third of the cost of shared transportation will be $37.75. However, given the density of traffic and the free spending mood of holiday crowds, she is planning on charging a price of $3.00.

Select Pricing: Breakeven Analysis from *The MART's* menu. Answer the following questions. When a change to the situation is introduced, begin from the situation described above. If your answer is a fraction, round to the next higher whole number.

Section_____   Name_____

                           Student Number_____

Select Pricing: Breakeven Analysis from *The MART* menu. Answer the following questions. When a change to the situation is introduced, begin from the situation described above. If your answer is a fraction, round to the next higher whole number.

1.   What is Ruth's breakeven point in units for this show?

      _____

2.   What is the BEP if there is a hidden charge of $75.00 for shopping center laborers and electricians to set up booths?

      _____

3.   What effect would it have if the charge for space were $500 plus 10% of sales?

      _____

4.   Diane, one of the people with whom Ruth expects to share a truck, can't raise the $500. Experience has shown that Saturday will be Ruth's best day, by far, and Friday will hardly be worth the effort. Diane's pottery has usually sold best on Sunday. She has proposed that Ruth pay the $500 and that she buy Friday and Sunday from Ruth for $100 each. The show managers don't like this sort of arrangement, but will go along if payment is by certified check and each party pays a $25 fee for "storage of temporarily unneeded inventory and fixtures." What would Ruth's breakeven point in units be under this arrangement? In dollars?

      Should Ruth accept this proposal rather than taking a booth for the entire weekend herself?

      _____

      _____

5. Ruth used her PC to integrate her experience relating sales to traffic with the Kris Kringle show's prediction of daily attendance and the franchiser's data on sales at various prices. The following forecasts of unit sales resulted.

Price	Sales
$2.00	900
2.50	650
3.00	450
3.25	400

Should Ruth charge her anticipated price of $3.00?

---

6. A fellow business student offered to help Ruth apply decision theory to her pricing problem. He would want a fee of $200 for helping her to choose among the four competing prices. Should Ruth accept?

---

7. Diane (see 4, above) sells a wide range of pottery items ranging from small novelties, such as spoon holders for use at the stove, to full sets of dinnerware. Her usual pricing practice is to estimate an item's cost and double that. What would her breakeven point be if she had to rent a space on her own for the full show? (Press <Esc> to return to menu and clear entries.)

What would it be if her proposal to buy Friday and Sunday from Ruth were accepted?

Diane is considering changing her markup to 80% of selling price during the holiday season, to see if her pottery still sells. What will her breakeven point be at these prices?

Three days

Friday and Sunday only.

---

37 BNW Publishers

BNW publishers specialized in books for small specialty markets. Customers were under the impression that BNW were the initials of the owner, Billy Williams. Actually, it was an in-house joke. BNW stood for Books Nobody Wants.

BNW had gone through a review by a management consulting firm. One of the recommendations had been that BNW get a handle on its costs and pricing. The consulting team felt that in some instances prices were unrealistically low, given the probable level of sales. They recommended that BNW determine the breakeven point at any price being considered, and compare that to the probable level of sales.

Williams was considering the price to be charged for a history of Valleydale during the five years immediately before the Revolutionary War. The book was expected to appeal to three groups of customers: civic boosters, residents whose names appeared therein and amateur historians interested in the period. Being a realist, Williams knew it wasn't of a quality that would appeal to professional historians or university libraries.

The book ran to 353 pages. BNW had advanced the author $3,000 to finance professional line drawings when the author's own art work proved to be of inadequate quality. Typesetting would run $35 a page. Printing and binding would come to $7.50 a copy. The price being considered is $50.00.

Assignment

Select Pricing: Breakeven Analysis from *The MART*'s menu. Answer the following questions. When a change to the situation is introduced, begin from the situation described above. If your answer is a fraction, round to the next higher whole number, unless you know where you can sell half a book.

1. What would the breakeven point for the project be?

   _____

2. What would the breakeven be at a price of $40.00?

   _____

3. Having learned how high his BEP was, Williams would like to get it down. Needing to sell the kind of numbers determined above just to break even on a project, doesn't appeal to him. He is considering desktop publishing which will lower his typesetting costs to $10 per page. What will his breakeven point be at the prices shown below?

   $50.00

   _____

   $40.00

   _____

   $35.00

   _____

   $25.00

   _____

4. The consulting team conducted a follow up visit to see if there were any questions concerning their recommendations. While there, they convinced Williams that they could develop demand estimates that would be of value in arriving at a price. They introduced Williams to the idea of multiple breakeven analysis. Their best estimates for the project under consideration are shown below. Determine the breakeven point for each price. What price should be chosen? (Assume desktop publishing)

Price	Unit Sales	Breakeven Point
$25.00	380	_____
$35.00	300	_____
$40.00	210	_____
$50.00	150	_____

Would you be willing to invest in a research study to refine the demand estimates, if the price were not excessive?

_____

_____

5. Williams mentioned his pricing problem to a local supermarket manager after a PTA meeting. This worthy scoffed at the idea of estimating demand and held forth on the virtues of markup pricing.

Does markup pricing eliminate the need to consider demand? Why or why not?

_____

_____

6. Regardless of your answer, what would BNW's BEP (in dollars) on this book be if it were typeset using desktop publishing and the markup on selling price (markon) were as shown below? (Press <Esc> to return to menu and clear entries.)

90%

_____

80%

_____

65%

_____

50%

_____

40%

_____

38 Quayside Souvenirs

After taking early retirement from a major retail chain, three things soon became apparent to Brian Weissman. First, time seemed to pass very slowly. All that leisure wasn't so great when there was no work from which it provided an escape. Second, his seemingly generous pension didn't go nearly as far as he had hoped. Even though he had paid off his mortgage before retiring, unexpected expenses kept putting a strain on the household budget. Finally, unless he started getting out of the house on a regular basis, he feared his wife was going to get out on a permanent basis.

Brian was considering the purchase of half interest in a small souvenir and novelty shop on the outskirts of Tampa, Florida. He thought operating the store well would require the presence of one of the owners, in addition to a full time clerk. His partner and he could divide up the time in the store, leaving each a considerable amount of time for travel and other retirement activities.

The current owner did not seem to be much of a merchant. Brian felt that his own experience in big league retail management would enable him to do a much better job. The business was priced about right for its current operating results and was in an excellent location. If one could substantially improve earnings, the price would prove to have been a bargain.

Brian and his prospective partner had two different appraisals done. Though they differed in assumptions about the magnitude and timing of possible improvements in operations, both indicated that the shop was worth the price.

Brian wanted to take one more look. He wanted to know how much they would have to sell just to break even. The *pro forma* statement used in the more conservative of the two appraisals is in Table 13.

Table 13 *Pro Forma* Income Statement

	Quayside Souvenirs *Pro Forma* Income Statement			
Sales	500,000		100.0%	
Cost of Sales	<u>205,000</u>		41.0	
Gross Margin		295,000		59. 0
Rent and Related				
Expenses	130,000		26.0	
Employment Cost –				
Clerk	12,000		2.4	
Interest and Carrying				
Charges	15,000		3.0	
Selling and				
Administrative	66,000		13.2	
Other Expenses	<u>35,500</u>		<u>7.1</u>	
		<u>258,500</u>		<u>51.7</u>
Profit		36,500		7.3

Assignment

Select Pricing: Breakeven Analysis from *The MART's* menu. Answer the following questions. When a change to the situation is introduced, begin from the situation described in the case.

1. What would the breakeven point be under the assumptions used by the appraiser?

    _____

2. The old owner averaged a gross margin of only 25%. What would the breakeven point be if Brian cannot improve upon that?

    _____

3. The present owner and his wife have staffed the store themselves. How much does hiring a clerk increase the breakeven point?

    _____

4. What would the breakeven point be if cost of goods sold could be reduced to 38%?

    _____

IX Channels of Distribution

In this Part we examine decisions made by channel members and the impact of these decisions on their profitability. First, we introduce a model around which the exercises and cases will be structured, the Dupont Model. Next follow exercises in which you observe the impact of changing gross margins on the income statements and balance sheets of firms in simulated competitive environments. The final cases involve applying the Dupont Model to the problems of organizations at the wholesale and retail levels.

39 The Dupont Model

The objective of this module, and the exercises and cases that follow, is to increase your understanding of the relationships among price, volume, financial decisions and profitability. To accomplish this, extensive use will be made of an old chestnut called the Dupont model, after the firm for which it was developed. This model can be very elaborate. Fortunately, the simple form shown below will serve our purpose.

$$\frac{Profit}{Sales} \times \frac{Sales}{Assets} \times \frac{Assets}{Equity} = \frac{Profit}{Equity} = Return\ on\ Equity\ (ROE)$$

Stated in words, Profit Margin X Asset Turnover X Leverage = ROE.

There is nothing magic here. If one simplifies the equation,

$$\frac{Profit}{Sales} \times \frac{Sales}{Assets} \times \frac{Assets}{Equity} = \frac{Profit}{Equity} = Return\ on\ Equity\ (ROE)$$

$$\frac{Profit}{Equity} = \frac{Profit}{Equity} = ROE$$

one sees that it is definitional. However the original form has the advantage of highlighting the factors contributing to return on equity (ROE).

Components

Depending on the purpose the profit margin may be gross or net. Asset turnover measures how hard the assets of a firm are working at producing sales. For a merchant, inventory is, typically, the most important asset. In such instances, this ratio is, for all practical purposes, the inventory turnover ratio. A value of six would indicate merchandise was moving through six times as quickly as a ratio of one. Factors under direct control of the merchant, such as gross margin, inventory level, service levels, skillful buying and store environment affect the value of this ratio.

The third ratio measures financial leverage, the degree to which a firm is using borrowed money to magnify the return on the owner's or shareholders' investment. A ratio of two would indicate that there are two dollars of assets for every dollar the owner(s) have invested.

204

These additional assets are supported by borrowing. Therefore, there is a dollar of debt for every dollar of equity.

Objective and Tradeoffs

In the best of all possible worlds, one would like high values for *all* terms to the left in order to realize the highest return. Unfortunately, the world doesn't work that way; there are tradeoffs. Normally, high margins and high prices result in lower sales and turnover. Beyond reasonable leverage values, borrowing costs become prohibitive and risk becomes unacceptable. Suppliers, aware of the level of debt, may refuse to deliver merchandise, forcing margin and turnover to zero. (Witness Federated Department Stores under Robert Campeau.)

The ratio on the right, return on equity, is the *objective* we usually think of maximizing. Even here caution is in order. An exceptionally high ROE might indicate that an additional infusion of equity is warranted, in order to increase dollar profit. If you're trying to support your college education from the earnings on your pushcart, even a 200% return on equity won't pay your fees, if you have only $100 invested.

40 The Effect of Gross Margin

The following exercises place several firms in a simulated environment. They are designed to allow you to explore the effects changing gross margin (prices) could have on the other variables in the Dupont model, keeping all else equal.

As you approach this part, keep in mind that, in a competitive environment, high margins can only be sustained by an extremely attractive offering. Providing this is, usually, expensive. Exclusive clothing stores have higher margins than Cheap Sam's Discount Clothes. They also have a higher cost structure. Cheap Sam's may be more profitable.

Many interactions are possible. The quantity of goods sold can influence the cost of goods sold (variable cost). If sales are low, one may have to purchase from less efficient wholesalers and will not benefit from quantity discounts and other economies of scale in purchasing. At extremely high levels channel capacity may be strained and suppliers may experience diseconomies of scale.

Sales levels and the cost of goods sold determine the dollar value of the average inventory. Since debt may be used to finance working capital needs, the value of the inventory can impact on one's leverage ratio, as well as overhead and administrative expenses.

To run these exercises, choose Channels: Part A from *The MART's* main menu. In each exercise you will have to make a judgment as to the effect changes in price will have on demand. Experiment with different values for Gross Margin and record the values for the other terms in the model. Try to find the value for Gross Margin which maximizes Return on Equity.

41 San Ramon Salt

Since medieval times, the Grand Dukes of San Ramon had held a monopoly on importing and selling salt. Profits from this enterprise were, historically, a significant source of revenues for the palace coffers. Since the building of a casino at the beginning of the twentieth century, gambling had replaced salt as the major income source. Selling salt had become a handy make-work project, providing well-paying, not very demanding jobs for those in favor with the reigning Grand Duke and his cabinet.

Following the revolution, a democratically elected government had "thrown the rascals out." State enterprises had either been put under professional management, or privatized. San Ramon Salt remained a state owned corporation and continued to enjoy a monopoly on salt.

San Ramon's manager, Guy La Sel, was charged with the responsibility of maximizing the return on the republic's investment. He is currently in the process of establishing a mark-up policy. Use Channels Part A to find a gross margin which will accomplish Mr. La Sel's mission.

Assignment

I believe price changes will have _____ effect on demand.

Gross Margin	Asset Turnover	Leverage	Return on Equity
_____	_____	_____	_____

1. What Gross Margin would you advise Mr. Sel to attempt to realize?

    _____

2. What would you recommend if the objective were changed to

    maximizing sales?

    _____

    maximizing dollar profits?

    _____

3. Explain your prediction as to the effects of price changes on demand.

    _____

    _____

42 Jim's General Store

Jim's General Store is a neighborhood convenience store. Although it is not affiliated with any of the major chains, it operates in a similar manner. Jim's carries a limited assortment of rapidly moving merchandise. It is able to charge higher prices than supermarkets, because of its convenient location and extended operating hours.

Jim is considering his average markup. If it is too low, he is providing geographical and temporal convenience at no cost to his customers, and sacrificing profit. If it is too high, customers will go to a competitor. He is seeking a markup policy which will maximize his return on equity. See if you can help him. Select Channels: Part A from *The MART's* menu.

Assignment

I believe price changes will have _____ effect on demand.

Gross Margin	Asset Turnover	Leverage	Return on Equity
_____	_____	_____	_____

1. What Gross Margin would you advise Jim to set?

   _____

2. What would you recommend if the objective were changed to

   maximizing sales?

   _____

   maximizing dollar profits?

   _____

3. Explain your prediction as to the effects of price changes on demand.

   _____

   _____

43 United Pushcart

United Pushcart was one of four firms engaged in street vending in Mountain View. Muriel Hope, the owner, was working on the business plan for food operations in the coming quarter. The food operation owns and operates vending wagons selling hot dogs, fries and other items requiring little on the spot preparation. Some of the wagons are leased to university students who operate them as independent businesses, while others are staffed by employees of United Pushcart. Regardless, all have identical assortments and prices.

Sales tend to concentrate at three times of day. Lunch is the busiest period, particularly during nice weather. Next comes the early morning hours when the bars and clubs close and exiting patrons are easily tempted by a quick bite to eat, if it's handy. Third in importance, is the after work period in the downtown office area.

United's carts always have one to three competitors at any site. While the competing firms attempt to differentiate their offering by varying condiments, etc., customer loyalty is low. Informal questioning of customers indicates that "cheap" and "handy" are the primary purchasing motives. "A dog's a dog."

To complete the business plan Muriel needed to set a target markup. Her objective was to maximize return on equity. Where should she set the average markup? Select Channels: Part A from *The MART's* menu to answer the following questions.

Section_____   Name_____

                                           Student Number_____

Assignment

I believe price changes will have _____ effect on demand.

<table>
<tr><td>Gross
Margin</td><td>Asset
Turnover</td><td>Leverage</td><td>Return on
Equity</td></tr>
<tr><td>_____</td><td>_____</td><td>_____</td><td>_____</td></tr>
</table>

1.   What Gross Margin would you advise Muriel to set?

     _____

2.   What would you recommend if the objective were changed to
     maximizing sales?

     _____

     maximizing dollar profits?

     _____

3.   Explain your prediction as to the effects of price changes on demand.

     _____

     _____

44 Using The Computer Model

When running Channels Part B, the Dupont Model will be displayed on the screen. You can change any individual value and the remaining values are automatically recalculated, so you can observe the impact of the change.

To run this model, choose Channels Part B from the main menu and follow the prompts. You will have to choose a case, or "User Input." If you choose a case, the model will automatically be initialized with case data. Choosing "User Input" allows you to input the values for any other problems which you wish to explore.

Cases vs User Input. The cases have built in demand functions relating sales to the price level implied by your selection of GM-%. Therefore, in some instances, values displayed after recalculation may not be exactly what you specified. Planning for sales of $1,000,000 does not mean that you will realize exactly $1,000,000. That's the way the world works. If you want to test an exact set of values, use the User Input mode.

Reinitializing. At several points, cases suggest that you return to the initial values for the variables. It is not necessary to type these in, again. Simply press < Esc > to return to the menu and reselect the case. The initial values will automatically be inserted into the model.

When the model is displayed, use the cursor keys to move around the screen. When a value you wish to change is highlighted press the < Pg Dn > key. Type the new values for the variable you are changing, then press < Enter >. Do not type commas, or percent, or dollar signs. These will be entered by the computer for ease of reading. Don't worry if you make a mistake. Values can be changed as many times as you wish.

To enhance flexibility, the model has been formulated slightly differently than in the introduction to the Dupont Model (p. 204). The numerator of the left hand (margin) term will appear as

(GM-$ - Expenses-$)
OR (GM-% - Expenses-%)

As indicated, you may input Gross Margin and expenses in either dollars or as a percent of sales. The other value ($ or %) will be calculated and displayed automatically. As in the real world, one cannot say for sure what the outcome of a decision will be. The advantage of this exercise is that it allows you to ask "what if" questions. For example, you may not be able to say for sure how sales will respond to a 5% increase in prices (GM). You can ask the question, "What will be the impact on ROE if GM increases and sales stay the same? decline 10%? decline 20%?, etc."

The model calculates profit as net profit after all expenses (selling, administrative and overhead), but before taxes. If you want to see some other value, this can be accomplished by changing the value input for expenses. For example, if you wish to look at gross profit, in dollars, simply set the percent expenses at zero. (This is the only place where the program will accept a value of zero.)

45 Krankenhaus Gifts

Krankenhaus Gifts, located in City Infirmary Hospital, serves the needs of patients, visitors and staff. The shop carries gift merchandise, flowers and flower arrangements, and an assortment of notions and health and beauty aids.

Krankenhaus is an activity of the City Infirmary Auxiliary, a nonprofit organization devoted to raising funds for the hospital. The hospital provides space, utilities, cleaning and maintenance. To date, Krankenhaus has been staffed and managed entirely by volunteers. Other than a few thousand dollars worth of fixtures and a cash register, inventory is the only asset. Since the store has no occupancy, selling or overhead expenses, nearly every dollar of gross profit flows directly to the bottom line and, ultimately, to the Auxiliary's annual contribution to the Hospital Equipment fund.

Problems

Performance

The volunteer managers serve in that capacity for a period of two years. Several factors have been concerning Mary Mattingly, the incumbent. Foremost among these is the level of performance in the recent past. (See Table 14.) Krankenhaus is about the same size and has roughly the same sort of merchandise as many small commercial gift stores. Yet the annual net profit has seldom been large enough to pay the rent and salaries that a commercial operation would have to pay, much less produce a return for the owner.

Further, performance has varied widely over time. In some years the profit has been less than what the Infirmary could have made by renting out the space. In those years the thousands of hours of volunteer time yielded an effective return of zero.

Management

A student group from a senior marketing class at Riverton University recently took on Krankenhaus as a Spring class project. In analyzing the problems mentioned above, they focused on the level and inconsistency, in the skills of the volunteer managers. Their primary recommendation was that the Auxiliary hire a full time manager for the shop. (This was viewed by some as self-serving. With the dollars available, the Auxiliary could just about pay the entry level salary of a newly graduated business major. Riverton U. had the only school of business in the metropolitan area.)

Buying

Buying also concerned Mary. When the shop was founded forty years ago there were no wholesalers in Riverton handling gift items. Several volunteers had begun making semi-annual buying trips to gift shows in major cities. Riverton had grown considerably and local suppliers had emerged. Mary felt that she could procure all the merchandise they needed from local wholesalers, catalogs and importer's sales people, who called regularly.

Table 14 Income Statements

	Krankenhaus Operations Year Ended February 28, 1989			
	1989	%	1990	%
Sales	163,307	100.0	156,974	100.0
Cost of Sales				
Beginning Inv.	28,815		19,094	
Purchases	126,923		119,503	
Goods Available for Sale	155,738		138,597	
Ending Inv.	36,153		28,815	
Cost of Sales	119,585	73.2	109,782	69.9
Gross Profit	43,722	26.8	47,192	30.1
Expenses				
General Admin	2,520		3,765	
Buying Trips	3,307		2,867	
Total	5,827	3.6	6,632	4.2
Net Income	37,895	23.2	40,560	25.8

Krankenhaus was the only shop, profit or nonprofit, in Riverton that *really* did most of its buying at the gift shows. The owners and managers of several Riverton gift shops made the trip to Chicago, New York or Toronto, taking along their spouses to "take advantage of their expert judgment." It was rumored that some interrupted their round of restaurant, nightclub and theater offerings long enough to look in at the show arena, but no one could prove it. Krankenhaus's buyers did go to the shows and do the buying. However, Mary wondered if this was a wise expenditure of money or volunteer time. The latter was an increasingly scarce resource.

Section_____   Name_____

                          Student Number_____

Assignment

Select Channels Part B: Full Dupont Model from *The MART's* menu. Use the Channels Module to complete the following questions and exercises. Several of the exercises involve judgment calls. In these instances there are no correct answers.

The model recalculates after each entry. Sales will change if you change gross margin, reflecting a change in prices. Before accepting any answer, be sure the values you wish to use show for all entries.

1.   The Dupont Model introduced at the beginning of this section is contained in the Channels Module. Call the Krankenhaus data. Play with the model for a bit to see what happens when you change the various parameters.

2.   Press < Esc > and reinitialize with the values for Krankenhaus. Evaluate the proposal to employ a full time manager. Assume the manager can directly affect some of the ratios in the model. How much of a change is necessary to justify this proposal, if the total employment cost (salary and benefits) would be $25,000?

      Gross Margin would have to change

      From _____ To _____ ,

      if sales remain unchanged.

      Asset Turnover would have to change

      From _____ To _____ ,

      (Consider assets (inventory) to be fixed at $50,000.)

      How could a manager increase Gross Margin?

      _____

      _____

      _____

What sorts of things would increase asset turnover?

_____

_____

_____

Is there a conflict between these two strategies?

_____

_____

_____

3.   The buying trips will cost Krankenhaus about $5,000 next year. Do you think they
      should be discontinued? What assumptions did you make? Manipulate the model to see
      what values for Sales, Gross Margin, or Turnover justify your answer.

Decision

_____

Assumptions

_____

_____

_____

Values

_____

_____

_____

4. Krankenhaus engages in straight markup pricing, charging whatever is considered traditional for different types of merchandise. Markups vary from 25% to 50% of selling price. Item prices are frequently lowered when it is pointed out that a mass merchandiser sells the same item for less on a regular (not leader) basis.

    Standard markup pricing cannot be supported on theoretical grounds, since it ignores the effect of price on customer demand. How do you feel about it in Krankenhaus's case?

    _____

    _____

    _____

    If you managed Krankenhaus and had decided to use markup pricing, would you set your prices at, above, or below those charged by conventional retailers in Riverton? (The hospital is somewhat isolated and parking is difficult.)

    _____

    _____

    Should the shop continue to cut prices to meet those of the mass merchandisers? Why?

    _____

    _____

    _____

5. Mary is concerned about the year over year comparison shown in Table 14. Sales increased, yet profits declined. What must have happened?

    _____

    _____

Mary's predecessor held the shop's first sale in the most recent year shown, cutting prices on slow moving and non-moving inventory until it sold. Could this have contributed to last year's results? How?

_____

_____

_____

46 Main Street Grocery

Sam Stangler, a successful lawyer, had recently bought the Main Street Grocery and was pondering its fate. The store was located in a Victorian era residential area immediately adjacent to the downtown core. The neighborhood had declined severely during the post WW II rush to the suburbs. It was, now, turning around rapidly. Older couples, who tired of mowing the grass after their children were raised, and young professionals were discovering the advantages of living adjacent to the revitalized central shopping and entertainment district.

The Store and Building

The grocery was just an old neighborhood store of the sort that is largely out of favor. The building housed selling space, storage space and a large apartment on the second floor that had been occupied by the former owners. It was a little run down, but there were no structural problems and it could be easily spruced up.

The grocery business was another matter. Records were in a total state of disarray. The former owners had so commingled their own affairs with those of the store, that neither Sam nor his accountant ever did get it all shaken out. He figured that they had made a living and not much more in the recent past.

Sam had never been a storekeeper and didn't want to become one. He had bought the property speculating on rising prices. He figured that the price he had paid was justified by the value of the lot, alone. If something could be salvaged from the building and the business, that would be a bonus.

Sam would have liked to have sold the store as a going concern, and collected rent on the store space from the buyer. Renting the apartment would be no problem. However, a willing buyer had yet to be found for the grocery and it did not look as if one was going to appear. This left Sam considering three alternatives.

Alternatives

Write It Off. First, he could simply write off the grocery as a going concern and rent the space to others, probably a retailer of some sort, to use as they wished. This would be the least hassle solution. Unfortunately, after a brief survey of the rental market, it looked as if the combined rents on the apartment and retail space would fall somewhat short of the interest payments on the mortgage, leaving him out of pocket by the amount of taxes and maintenance costs. He could handle the negative cash flow, but thought he could do better.

Professional Management. The other alternatives involved Sam owning a retail business occupying the space. It seemed logical that it would be a food store, because that permitted use of some of the coolers and store fixtures on hand, as well as getting the most from the inventory he had purchased. The first thing that occurred to Sam was to hire an experienced store manager, perhaps from one of the franchised convenience stores, pay what the position was worth, and turn store management over to that person, entirely. Merchandise selection, inventory control, staffing and everything else would be the manager's responsibility. Since fewer clerks will be needed, a manager could probably be found for an increase in salary expense of $30,000.

Turn and Urn. The second possibility was suggested by a brochure he had received in the mail from an outfit called Turn and Urn, Inc. This company claimed to be able to maximize the performance of small, independent food stores. According to the brochure, their objective was to deliver many of the advantages of belonging to a convenience store chain without a lump sum franchise fee and at a lower charge against sales. They could not, of course, offer the advantages of a common identity and common promotion, which belonging to a chain conveyed.

Reading between the lines, it seemed that what was being offered was guidance as to merchandise assortment and an inventory management program, both designed to raise the gross margin and the turnover rate. Sam believed this program might be of interest, if he were willing to do a few things himself, like hiring and firing. The job of manager could be turned over to a glorified cashier, who could be hired for much less than the experienced store manager envisioned under the second alternative. Turn and Urn's fee was 2% of sales. Sam estimated that he could hire a more skilled clerk for one shift for an additional $2.00 per hour ($4,000 per year).

Pro Forma Statements

Sam's accountant worked out pro forma statements for the store merely to continue operating in its present mode, which are shown in Table 15. She assumed the store would be incorporated as a separate entity and, for purposes of analysis, should be charged with an appropriate rental for the space it occupied. She further assumed Sam would perform the managerial functions performed by the former owners, which didn't seem overly burdensome.

Table 15 Best Guess Statements for the *Status Quo*

Income Statement		Balance Sheet	
		Total Assets	$52,304
Sales	$220,210	Current Liabilities	17,783
Cost of Goods Sold	173,305	Long Term Debt	17,261
Gross Margin	46,905	Total Liabilities	35,044
Operating Expenses	47,345	Owners Equity	17,260
Net Profit	(440)	Total Liabilities and Net Worth	52,304

Assignment

Select Channels Part B: Full Dupont Model from *The MART's* menu. The model recalculates after each entry. Sales will change if you change gross margin, reflecting a change in prices. Before accepting any answer, be sure the values you wish to use show for all entries.

1. Assuming no improvements in store operations, what will the operating results of main street grocery be if Sam adds a professional manager at a cost of $30,000?

    Net Profit (Loss)_____

    What if he accepts the Turn and Urn proposal at a cost of $4,000 plus 2% of sales?

    Net Profit (Loss)_____

2. For either of the proposals to be viable, store operations must improve. Consider the Dupont model. How can management improve store operating results?

    _____

    _____

3. Assume a hired manager is charged with producing a 15% return on equity and decides to attempt to accomplish this by raising sales. How high would sales have to be? (Consider expenses, including the manager's salary, to be fixed at $77,345.)

    Sales_____

    Do the other ratios seem reasonable?

    Change assets, equity and sales so as to achieve a 15% return on equity while holding asset turnover to 6.0, or less, and leverage to less than, or equal to 2.0. This requires

    Sales _____

    Assets_____

    Equity_____

What could a manager do to raise sales?

_____

_____

_____

4.   Assume a hired manager is charged with producing a 15% return on equity and decides to attempt to accomplish this by increasing gross margin. How high would gross margin need to be? (Consider expenses, including the manager's salary, to be fixed at $77,345.)

Gross Margin-%_____

How could a manager increase gross margin?

_____

_____

5.   Turn and Urn promises to improve results by increasing gross margin and/or raising turnover. What would it take to produce a 15% return on equity by increasing gross margin? (Consider hiring a more skilled clerk and other expenses to be fixed at $51,345 plus 2 percent of sales.)

Gross Margin-%_____

How high would turnover have to be to produce a 15% return on equity?

_____

How can turnover be increased?

_____

_____

47 Barry-Pitcher Distributors

Barry-Pitcher Distributors was formed in 1983 as the result of the merger of Barry Foods and Pitcher Restaurant Supply. The firm attempts to be able to meet most of the purchasing needs of the away-from-home food service industry, with the exception of fresh meat and produce. Its lines include processed foods (69% of sales), restaurant equipment (17%) and paper products and cleaning supplies (14%). Approximately 20% of food items are manufactured in the company's own plants.

Growth Potential and Limitations

Barry-Pitcher's customers include restaurants and institutional food service operations ranging from airlines to industrial cafeterias to prisons. Its 24 distribution centers serve the needs of customers in 37 states.

Meal service away from home is one of the most rapidly growing segments of the economy. In 1989 one in three meals was eaten away from home. This is expected to grow to a full 50% by the turn of the century. A growing proportion of these meals is served by the national chains that are Barry-Pitcher's major customers. One hundred firms accounted for forty percent of the meals served by the food service industry.

Barry finds its growth potential in its present markets hampered by the lack of complete coverage of the 48 contiguous states. The large institutional food service companies prefer to deal with suppliers who can serve their needs in all markets.

Alternatives

The firm has followed a policy of leasing space for its distribution centers whenever possible, thus minimizing its investment in bricks and mortar. The alternatives for growth under consideration will require various additions to the firm's fixed asset base, resulting in a very different looking balance sheet.

Merger

Barry fully serviced both coasts, the sunbelt and the inter-mountain states. It did not operate in the Great Lakes region or the central states. Established competitors in this region were large, sophisticated, and had a strong customer franchise. Barry–Pitcher management had always viewed the risks of an attempt to penetrate the area as greater than the gains to be realized in the region, taken alone. The growing desirability of becoming a fully national supplier cast a different light on the subject.

Midwest Restaurant Supply, a privately held corporation owned by Jerome Kirtchner and his family, was on the block for the right buyer. Midwest is, except for geographical location, just a one-third slice of Barry–Pitcher, and for good reason. Jerome had adopted Barry–Pitcher as his strategic planning department. Whatever the larger firm did, Midwest copied, on its own scale. Barry–Pitcher moved into processed foods, Jerome went into processed foods. Barry–Pitcher added equipment, Midwest went into equipment, etc., etc.

Kirtchner and his brothers have reached that stage in life at which estate planning is of more concern than managing a company. None of their heirs are active in the company nor do they have an interest in becoming so. Midwest's shares are all held by family members and a market value is difficult to determine. The whole family would welcome a friendly merger with a company, such as Barry–Pitcher, traded on a major exchange.

Discussions between Barry–Pitcher and the Kirtchners had reached the point where the larger firm had to either make a commitment or back away. It looked extremely promising. The firms fit like a hole in a doughnut. The Kirtchner's would take a package of debentures and common stock. The deal would be arranged so as to neither dilute the earnings of existing stockholders nor substantially raise Barry–Pitcher's borrowing costs for working capital and replacing existing bonds, as they came due.

Barry–Pitcher's management estimated that merely becoming a fully national firm would add 25% to their sales in the areas Barry–Pitcher already served. The only drawback was that the Kirtchners insisted on very restrictive bond covenants that would make further acquisitions or major expansions extremely unlikely.

Product Mix

Equipment carries considerably higher margins (31%) than food products (14%), or paper products (17%). Barry–Pitcher's sales mix had remained unchanged for a decade and the constitution and emphasis of the sales force had remained constant. Marketing executives believed profitability would be enhanced by raising equipment sales to 50% of sales, from the present 17%, and that such a move was feasible.

Achieving a new sales mix would not be accomplished without monetary and organizational costs. A no-growth state would have to be accepted for the food and supplies lines, with all free resources going into the equipment business. More and higher level salespersons would need to be hired. Service facilities would have to be expanded. More repair and service personnel would be required.

This alternative will cause an increase in expenses to over 18% of sales. The investment costs will have to be financed by debt, which may raise Barry–Pitcher's overall borrowing costs.

Manufacturing

Barry–Pitcher now manufactures 20% of the food items it sells. If this proportion could be raised, the firm would benefit by capturing both the manufacturer's and the wholesaler's margins on the goods. This is particularly attractive, since food processing, generally, carries a higher net profit than wholesaling.

To date, food processing had been pretty much a sideline. Having decided a distribution center was warranted in an area, Barry–Pitcher would occupy (lease if possible) a manufacturing plant, if one was available at an attractive price, and co-locate the operations.

Analysis of food sales indicates that 70% self-manufacturing is about the upper limit. This will raise Barry–Pitcher's gross margin to nearly 25%. The projected investment in plant and equipment would have to be financed by taking on additional debt. This may lower the rating on the firm's debentures, raising its debt service costs.

Pro Forma Statements

The strategic planning committee, with inputs from various departments, has worked out *pro forma* statements for each of the three alternatives, for a date five years in the future. (Table 16) Whatever alternative is adopted, it will be fully implemented by that time. The competitive environment, coupled with shareholder discontent over what is viewed as an excessive cash position, render continuing the *status quo* a non-starter.

Table 16 Comparisons of Three Alternatives

Operating Statement (000's)

	Merger with Midwest		Build Sales Of Equipment		Increase Food Manufacturing	
Sales	2,054,000	100.0%	2,158,000	100.0%	1,300,000	100.0%
Cost of Goods Sold	1,694,550	82.5	1,687,556	78.4	981,500	75.5
Gross Margin	359,450	17.5	470,444	21.6	318,500	24.5
Expenses	287,560	14.0	388,440	18.0	239,200	18.4
Net Profit	71,890	3.5	82,004	3.6	79,300	6.1

Balance Sheet (000's)

Assets			
Current	581,709	580,834	384,890
Fixed	28,633	43,058	71,365
Total	610,342	623,892	456,255
Liabilities and Owners' Equity			
Liabilities			
Current	129,501	240,834	44,890
Long Term	90,581	89,629	117,936
Total	220,082	330,463	162,826
Owners' Equity	390,260	293,429	293,429
Total	610,342	623,892	456,255

Assignment

Select Channels Part B: Full Dupont Model from *The MART's* menu. Use the User Input option to complete the following exercises.

The model recalculates after each entry. Before accepting an answer be sure the values you wish to use show for all entries.

1. Complete the missing entries in the table.

GM-%	Exp	Sales	Assets	Equity	Profit	Profit %	Turn-over	Lever-age	ROE
17.5	14.0	2,054,000	610,342	390,260	71,890	3.5	3.4	1.6	18.4
20.5	17.0	2,054,000	610,342	390,260	____	____	____	____	____
21.0	14.0	2,054,000	610,342	390,260	____	____	____	____	____
17.5	14.0	4,108,000	610,342	390,260	____	____	____	____	____
17.5	14.0	2,054,000	305,172	390,260	____	____	____	____	____
17.5	14.0	2,054,000	305,172	195,130	____	____	____	____	____

What does this table illustrate?

_____

2. Which of the three alternatives under consideration at Barry-Pitcher will yield the highest return on equity?

_____

3. Try different gross margins for the merger. At what level does this alternative show the highest return on equity?

_____

4. Barry's short term debt is financed at prime plus one percent. Interest rates are expected to be extremely volatile over the planning period. What impact would the increases shown below have on the relative desirability of the three alternatives being considered? (Increases of the magnitudes shown may not seem believable. Yet, even a 10% increase would result in borrowing costs lower than the firm experienced in the early eighties.)

Interest Rate Increase	Merger	Resulting in Expenses of Build Sales of Equipment	Increase Food Manufacturing
2%	290,150	393,257	240,098
5	294,035	400,482	241,444
10	300,510	412,523	243,689

_____

_____

5. Assume that the merger had to be entirely debt financed, as was the case with the other alternatives. This would result in expenses of $297,000. Equity would be $293,429, as in the other two alternatives (000 omitted). What would the return on equity have been?

_____

6. Barry-Pitcher is not known for having a firm hand on expenses. How much of a reduction in expenses would it take to make increasing manufacturing the most desirable alternative?

_____

7. The merger alternative shows a considerably lower gross margin than the others. How much would this have to increase, as a percent of sales, for the merger to have the highest ROE?

_____

8. Assume that there is the possibility of an infusion of $100 million of new equity for the manufacturing alternative. What level of sales would have to result in order to maintain return on equity?

_____

X Physical Distribution

Having chosen the channel, or channels through which our products will be made available to the consumer, there remains a set of decisions concerning the manner and timing of moving the goods themselves. How much to ship, when, by what mode and whether or not they accumulate at stops along the way as inventories, are physical distribution decisions.

The cases and exercises that follow are designed to help you understand various aspects of physical distribution management.

Physical Distribution Evolves

The Dark Ages

Managerial thinking about physical distribution has undergone a radical change in recent decades. Originally, physical distribution activities were looked upon as resulting in a set of unrelated costs which must be borne, akin to sweeping the plant floors and mowing the grass in front of company headquarters. Inventory, warehousing and transportation activities were viewed as independent; decisions concerning these matters were often made by different managers. The related expenses were simply costs to be minimized, individually.

Total Cost Concept

The first step forward was the recognition that physical distribution activities were part of an integrated system with many interactions. If one uses a cheaper and slower mode of transportation, then inventory is increased, as a minimum, by the increase in the average amount of inventory in transit. Using more warehouses will entail either higher inventories, or shipments in smaller, less economical quantities. The *total cost concept* recognized these interactions among the various costs and took as an objective minimizing total cost, rather than the individual costs.

Physical Distribution Concept

The total cost concept assumed that customers were indifferent among physical distribution alternatives. The *physical distribution concept* recognizes that customers have legitimate preferences for more rapid, more reliable deliveries, fresh merchandise, lower spoilage and breakage, etc. The physical distribution concept identifies these features, collectively, as the *customer service level* and considers them to be an integral part of the marketing mix.

An improved customer service level can attract customers just as can product quality, advertising, or low prices. The objective of physical distribution decisions is seen as minimizing distribution costs, *subject to* maintaining a predetermined customer service level.

The Physical Distribution Program

The physical distribution program contains five subprograms of varying complexity. These will allow you to explore many aspects of physical distribution management.

EOQ Tutorial

The *Economic Order Quantity* (EOQ) formula is an important element in many physical distribution models. It enables one to determine how much to order at one time, based on information about annual demand, the cost of placing an order, and the cost of carrying a unit of inventory for one year. The quantity ordered at one time influences the number of orders placed in a year, the interval between orders and average inventory levels.

The EOQ Tutorial is a graphic demonstration of how EOQ responds to each of the factors that go into its determination. First, the way each of the costs responds to changes in order size is presented. Next, each of the factors entering the calculation is allowed to vary, holding the others constant, and the EOQ is plotted.

EOQ Calculations

The EOQ tutorial did not allow for user input. In this exercise, you will have the opportunity to enter values for each of the variables affecting the EOQ. The program will solve the problem, and display the EOQ, average inventory and annual costs.

The EOQ formula is

$$EOQ = \sqrt{\frac{2 * D * OC}{IC}}$$

where D = annual demand in units, OC = the cost of placing an order, IC = the cost of carrying a unit inventory for one year.

IC may be determined by multiplying the cost of one unit by the carrying cost expressed as a proportion.

Inventory Simulation

This exercise will allow you to experience the challenge of inventory management. You must try to meet customer demand while controlling inventory costs. When you run the program, you will first be presented with a screen requesting values for the following variables.

Annual Demand: The estimated number of units of product to be sold during the next 12 month period.

244

Ordering Cost: The cost, in dollars, of placing one order.

Cost per Item: The cost, in dollars, of one unit of product.

Carrying Cost: The cost of carrying a unit of the product in inventory for one year expressed as a *percentage* of the item's cost.

Safety Stock: Safety stock protects against delays in the delivery of orders, suppliers being unable to fill orders on time, surges in demand, and other unexpected events. If none of these occur, then safety stock becomes a permanent minimum inventory level.

If inventory drops below the level established for safety stock, then an emergency order will be placed by the program. Emergency orders are twice as costly to process as ordinary orders and have higher shipping costs.

Units Each Order: The number of units of product to be ordered at one time. If set too large, then inventory will build up. If too small a value is selected, then you will have to place many orders and will experience frequent stockouts and a high level of lost sales.

Inventory Control Systems

The program will permit either periodic or perpetual inventory control systems. In a *periodic inventory control system*, the inventory level is checked only periodically, at intervals you select, say weekly or monthly. Emergency orders are issued only if the inventory level drops to zero.

In the *perpetual inventory control system* the inventory level is checked after meeting each day's demand. If it falls below the order point — discussed below — resupply is ordered. If the inventory level is below the level set for safety stock, an emergency order is issued. The perpetual control system is more expensive than periodic control, but should result in lower inventories for a given customer service level.

Choosing a System

The inventory control system to be applied is triggered by entries for Order Point and Order Interval. If only an order point is entered, the program will apply perpetual inventory control. If the program is given non-zero values for both Order Point and Order Interval, it will use a periodic system. To change from periodic to perpetual, set Order Interval to zero.

Order Point: When inventory is checked and found to be below this value, an order is placed for the number of units you entered for order quantity.

Order Interval: The number of days between inventory checks. If inventory level is checked and found to be below the order point, an order is issued for the Order Quantity. Emergency orders are issued only to replenish safety stock, if inventory falls to zero.

Don't worry if you make a mistake. Any value may be changed by moving the cursor to the appropriate location and entering the new value.

Running the Inventory Simulation

When you have entered all values, press the <End> key. The program will simulate 12 months of operation and then issue a report. The top half of the report displays the values you entered. This is merely a reminder. Values such as carrying costs do not reflect added costs arising from perpetual inventory control, or the higher costs of transporting emergency orders.

Results

The outcomes resulting from your decisions are printed on a magenta background in the bottom portion. When you are satisfied with the solution, you may wish to obtain a printout using the <Shift-Prt Sc> keys.

The calculations of sales and lost sales assume a 50% markup on selling price. This percentage is higher than normal for the products in the cases. It was chosen because it facilitates mental calculations while using the program.

You will have three options when you have finished examining the output screen. 1) You may return to the input screen and change one or more of the values. The values of variables you do not change remain as originally entered. 2) You may run an entirely different inventory simulation problem. All values will be reset to zero. 3) You may return to the physical distribution menu.[1]

---

[1]The program has built-in assumptions about the variability of demand and the length and variability of delivery time. It should not be used to solve problems other than the cases.

Distribution Cost Tradeoffs

The objective of this exercise is to demonstrate the tradeoffs among the various components of total distribution cost. Simply enter the values in the proper location. Press <End> to calculate results. The program will determine the Economic Order Quantity (EOQ) and calculate a year's shipping and carrying costs, assuming orders are for EOQ-size lots.

After the results are displayed you may make changes to any entry and recalculate. Notice how the relative desirability of the transportation modes responds to the values you provide.

Physical Distribution Simulation

This simulation allows the user to choose any or all of the following changes to an on-going physical distribution system.

Inventory Locations: Add one, two, or three inventory storage sites at optimally chosen locations. The program does not differentiate among buying, or leasing a facility, or using public warehousing. As the number of sites increases, delivery time will fall; the customer service level will rise, as will inventory level and inventory carrying cost.

Transport Mode: Three levels of improvement over regular rail are offered for consideration. Each presumes the use of the lower — slower — levels when that will achieve equivalent results at lower cost. For example, even if one were willing to consider air freight, it would not be chosen if air freight and a cheaper mode both resulted in delivery on the next business day.

The possible transportation improvements are:

Improved Rail — Use the ExpiRail service offered by a consortium of carriers. The service promises closer monitoring of a shipment's progress than conventional rail, which results in less time spent on sidings and in switchyards.

Highway — Use trucks if they improve customer service levels or reduce costs.

Air Freight — This will be used as the regular mode in some cases and for rush or fill-in orders in others. Attractive rates might be negotiated for broader use where carriers have excess capacity.

Speed Order Entry: Reduce the time lag from when an order is received at headquarters to its arrival at the point from which shipment will be made.

The alternatives here are:

Add Order Clerks — Increase capacity to handle orders by present methods.

Internal Automation — Computerize processing from the time an order is received until it arrives at the point (warehouse) from which the goods will be shipped.

Automate Order Entry — Allow salespersons and regular customers to enter orders directly into the system. This step would include internal automation.

Speed Order Filling: Reduce the time from the arrival of an order at the shipping point to its departure.

Add Stock Handlers — Increase capacity to fill orders by current methods.

Mechanize — Purchase forklifts, etc.

Automate Order Filling — Computerize inventory storage sites. Install equipment for automated order picking.

Lower Stockout Probability: Increase inventory size. Change inventory controls and policies to reduce the probability of an item being out of stock to 10%, 5%, or 2%.

48 Economic Order Quantity (EOQ) Tutorial

Choose the EOQ Tutorial from *The MART's* menu. Repeat the tutorial until you understand how the various factors interact and how they impact on the EOQ.

Component Costs

As Quantity per order increases, ordering cost per unit (increases) (decreases)

(linearly) (exponentially) (other).

As Quantity per order increases, carrying cost per unit (increases) (decreases)

(linearly) (exponentially) (other).

As Quantity per order increases, total cost per unit (increases) (decreases)

(linearly) (exponentially) (other).

EOQ

As Carrying Cost per unit increases, EOQ (increases) (decreases)

(linearly) (exponentially) (other).

As Ordering Cost per unit increases, EOQ (increases) (decreases)

(linearly) (exponentially) (other).

As Annual Demand increases, EOQ (increases) (decreases)

(linearly) (exponentially) (other).

49 1–Stop Stores(A)

The 1–Stop chain promoted itself as low cost suppliers of the careful shopper's routine needs. The stores featured a supermarket, nonfashion apparel, minor appliances, furniture and hardware under a single roof. In 1989 the chain had almost gone into bankruptcy. Analysts blamed poor buying practices, which resulted in excess inventory expenses.

Formerly, individual buyers had determined order quantities and ordering frequency, largely flying by the seat of their pants. (Many crashed). You have been assigned the task of rationalizing ordering policies for a set of products. Ordering costs vary widely since the task ranges all the way from computers talking to computers to buying trips to trade shows and fairs.

Assignment

Choose the EOQ Calculations option from *The MART's* Physical Distribution menu. Complete the following table.

Item	Annual Demand Units	Cost per Unit	Ordering Cost per Order	Carrying Cost Percent	EOQ	Average Inventory	Annual Carrying Cost	Annual Ordering Cost	Total Cost
14" Portable Color TV	332	$301	$500	25	____	____	____	____	____
Woman's Shirt Dress	1,923	52	100	25	____	____	____	____	____
Two Piece Dress	2,173	46	100	25	____	____	____	____	____
10" Aviator Boot	1,515	66	50	17	____	____	____	____	____
Crew Neck Sweater	2,222	45	50	20	____	____	____	____	____
Lady's Blazer	2,325	53	500	25	____	____	____	____	____
Motorized Jogger	174	574	1,000	22	____	____	____	____	____
Snowsuit	2,380	42	10	10	____	____	____	____	____
3 Drawer Chest	446	224	100	20	____	____	____	____	____
Boy's Jacket[2]	5,882	17	10	17	____	____	____	____	____
Mirror	4,166	24	10	25	____	____	____	____	____

continued p. 252

---

[2]Product to be used in 1–Stop(B)

Item	Annual Demand Units	Cost per Unit	Ordering Cost per Order	Carrying Cost Percent	EOQ	Average Inventory	Annual Carry-ing Cost	Annual Order-ing Cost	Total Cost
Triple Curtain Rod	10,000	10	5	15	___	___	___	___	___
Skirt: Adhesive Closing	5,263	19	100	17	___	___	___	___	___
Latex Backed Rugs	2,857	35	5	15	___	___	___	___	___
Night Table	1,298	77	100	20	___	___	___	___	___
Bedroom Suite	204	490	500	25	___	___	___	___	___
Corduroy Skirt	3,225	31	10	20	___	___	___	___	___
Girl's Bodysuit	11,000	9	2	15	___	___	___	___	___
17 Cu Ft Refrigerator	170	588	500	20	___	___	___	___	___
Mock T-neck Sweater	3,703	27	10	20	___	___	___	___	___
Single Control Faucet	980	102	200	20	___	___	___	___	___
Youth's Denim Jackets	2,380	42	5	17	___	___	___	___	___
Men's Wool Sweaters	2,857	35	50	20	___	___	___	___	___

50 1-Stop Stores(B)

The 1-Stop Chain implemented your solutions to its order quantity problems. In most instances they seemed be an adequate solution. In others, variability in demand and/or delivery time resulted in either out of stock conditions and lost sales, or mounting inventories and excess carrying costs. It appeared that a more hands-on approach was warranted for these products.

The Boy's Jacket has proven to be a particularly troublesome product. Daily sales range from 0 to 32. Delivery times are relatively normally distributed around an average of 16 days. Part of this variability reflects the fact that the supplier operates on a five day a week schedule; an order received on Friday afternoon cannot possibly be shipped before Monday. (1-Stop is open and sends orders, by Fax, 365 days a year.) Emergency orders are costly, but arrive in an average of four days.

Assignment

Part A

Complete the following items using the values for the Boy's Jacket in 1–Stop Stores(A) (p. 252).

1. How many orders will be placed in a year, if one orders the EOQ each time?

   _____

2. If orders are placed at regular intervals, how many days' supply will be purchased with each order?

   _____

3. Suppose you wished to establish a safety stock equal to 10 days' sales. How many units would be in safety stock?

   _____

4. What is the cost of carrying the safety stock determined above for one year, if it is never needed to meet sales?

   _____

Part B

Choose Physical Distribution, then the Inventory Simulation from *The MART's* menus.

1. Try a wide range of values for order quantity, using an order point of 100 and safety stock of 0. What happens to sales and costs as you change order quantity? Are there tradeoffs, or can a value be found that minimizes both ordering cost and carrying cost.

Order Quant.	Sales $	Lost Sales $	Out of Stock Days	Ordering Cost (a)	Carrying Cost (b)	Total (a + b)
____	____	____	____	____	____	____
____	____	____	____	____	____	____
____	____	____	____	____	____	____
____	____	____	____	____	____	____
____	____	____	____	____	____	____

_____

_____

2. Test several different order points, using an order quantity of 200 and safety stock of 0. How does the order point affect costs, sales and lost sales?

Order Point	Sales $	Lost Sales $	Out of Stock Days	Ordering Cost (a)	Carrying Cost (b)	Total (a + b)
____	____	____	____	____	____	____
____	____	____	____	____	____	____
____	____	____	____	____	____	____
____	____	____	____	____	____	____
____	____	____	____	____	____	____

_____

_____

3. Test several different levels of safety stock, using an order quantity of 200 and an order point of 0. How does the amount of safety stock affect costs, sales and lost sales?

Safety Stock	Sales $	Lost Sales $	Out of Stock Days	Ordering Cost (a)	Carrying Cost (b)	Total (a + b)
___	___	___	___	___	___	___
___	___	___	___	___	___	___
___	___	___	___	___	___	___
___	___	___	___	___	___	___
___	___	___	___	___	___	___

_____

_____

4. Try a periodic inventory control system by entering several different values for order interval. Use an order quantity of 200, an order point of 100 and safety stock of 0. How does the order interval affect costs, sales and lost sales?

Order Interval	Sales $	Lost Sales $	Out of Stock Days	Ordering Cost (a)	Carrying Cost (b)	Total (a + b)
___	___	___	___	___	___	___
___	___	___	___	___	___	___
___	___	___	___	___	___	___
___	___	___	___	___	___	___
___	___	___	___	___	___	___

_____

_____

5. 1-Stop only makes money on sales. Is sales, alone a satisfactory standard for judging performance? What justification is there for monitoring lost sales, or out of stock days?

    _____

6. What criterion would you apply to judge the most desirable levels on any of the four decision variables examined above?

    _____

7. Run the simulation again using perpetual inventory control (order interval = 0). Test different values for order quantity, order point and safety stock. Record the values producing the most satisfactory results according to the criterion you selected above.

        order quantity   _____

        order point   _____

        safety stock   _____

8. Rerun the simulation again using periodic inventory control (order interval = 0). Test different values for order quantity, order point, safety stock and order interval. Record the values producing the most satisfactory results according to the criterion you selected above.

        order quantity   _____

        order point   _____

        safety stock   _____

        order interval   _____

51 Bardleigh Wholesale Office Supply

Bardleigh handled a wide range of office supplies and furniture. The firm sold to major institutional end users and office supply stores throughout the tri-state area. Billy Bob Bardleigh had recently become manager upon his father's retirement. It is Saturday afternoon and he would rather be at the lake fishing. Instead, he is at his desk establishing inventory policies for some products that have presented problems in the recent past.

One of these is the Commander, a popular desk/hutch used as a computer work station. Bardleigh sold about ten of these a week, though there was considerable season to season and week to week variation. Each of these desks cost Bardleigh $219. Delivery times ranged from five days to over three weeks, though rush orders could take as little as four days, if Bardleigh was willing to pay the added cost of this service.

Bardleigh was a favored customer at the First National Bank and financed its working capital needs at the prime lending rate plus one percent. A few years ago an accounting firm's study had indicated that the firm's inventory carrying cost for furniture products was 23% per year. Little had changed in the interim except that the prime had risen from 6.5% to 10.5%. The same study estimated the cost of placing an order at $50. Thanks to automation, this was believed to be appropriate today, in spite of soaring wage costs.

Section_____

Name_____

Student Number_____

Assignment

Choose Physical Distribution, then the Inventory Simulation from *The MART's* menus.

1. Try a *periodic* inventory control system, testing different values for units each order, safety stock, order point and order interval. Record the values producing the most satisfactory results.

      order quantity   _____

      order point   _____

      safety stock   _____

      order interval   _____

2. Repeat 1, using a *perpetual* inventory control system.

      order quantity   _____

      order point   _____

      safety stock   _____

3. What criterion did you use in determining the most satisfactory results? Can you think of others?

_____

_____

4. How would the return of the inflation levels of the early 80's and a 20.5% prime rate affect your answer to 2?

      order quantity   _____

      order point   _____

      safety stock   _____

5. What would your solution to 2 have been if the product under consideration were the Admiral? It is a superior product costing twice as much. Bardleigh sells about 250 per year.

order quantity _____

order point _____

safety stock _____

52 J. K. Thompson Enterprises

Jon Thompson is a sales agent, selling a variety of products to building supply wholesalers and retail chains in the Southwest. He is employed by manufacturers who desire representation in the area, but whose sales volume is not large enough to justify serving their customers with their own sales force. Jon's specialty is in not specializing. He represents a diverse set of manufacturers and attempts to maintain a balance between routine products, where he almost acts as an ordertaker, and items requiring more creative selling.

Thompson offers the manufacturers he represents a wide variety of services. Among these is recommending the mode of transportation to be used for shipments. He had always just used the cheapest mode, since the purchaser paid shipping from the manufacturer's warehouse (FOB plant). However, a customer recently complained that the savings arising from this practice were often more than offset by increased inventory carrying costs. This had become increasingly apparent as interest rates rose.

Jon agreed to look into the problem. The complaining customer provided a list of estimates of inventory carrying costs that he had received from a trade association. Jon drew a sample of orders he had recently processed. He then sorted the information on characteristics, such as distance and miles shipped, so that he could see how the relative desirability of transportation modes responded to changes in factors describing the shipment.

Assignment

Choose Physical Distribution, then Distribution Cost Tradeoffs from *The MART's* menus.

1. Jon's data is shown below. Determine the transportation mode which results in the cheapest total (shipping + carrying) cost for the customer for each item.

Item	Annual Demand	Average Distance	Cost per Unit	Carrying Cost – %	Weight per Unit	Preferred Mode
Garbage Disposers	200	6,000	$140	25	20	_____
Water Heaters	500	3,000	350	20	200	_____
Steel Garage Doors	100	5,000	800	40	300	_____
Exterior Doors	250	6,000	520	25	100	_____
Acrylic Bathtubs	300	3,000	100	17	40	_____
Deluxe Toilets	100	4,500	220	20	125	_____
Microwave Ovens	50	6,000	280	25	30	_____
Adj. Dado Blades	75	2,000	95	20	2	_____
Electronic Home Security Systems	30	6,500	280	25	11	_____
Smoke Alarms	400	4,900	24	17	1	_____

2. Are there factors other than annual cost that you would want to consider in selecting a transport mode?

_____

_____

3. The program assumes a single mode will be used from the shipping point to the purchaser's receiving dock. Is this appropriate?

_____

_____

     J. K. THOMPSON ENTERPRISES

53 Affiliated Dry Goods

Affiliated Dry Goods is a large, general merchandise, mail order retailer. The President, recently promoted from Vice President Finance, has been on a cost cutting crusade and has recently concentrated his wrath on physical distribution costs. His predecessor had been content to leave such matters to "the gnomes in green eyeshades," who simply attempted to minimize the cost of freight-in. Carrying costs had not been broken out by item, but simply appeared under general and administrative expense.

Affiliated recently opened a new warehouse and mailing center. The facility's capacity exceeded Affiliated's storage needs, but excess space could almost always be rented to others. Thanks to a booming local economy, there was an almost chronic shortage of warehouse space in the metro area. As a result of this situation, Affiliated's storage costs are almost entirely variable.

You were appointed to prepare a report on "Opportunities in Physical Distribution." As a first step you, with the help of a consultant, developed estimates of inventory carrying costs for a variety of products. The transportation manager has provided you with estimates of the costs and time involved in shipping various quantities of these goods typical distances.

Section_____   Name_____

Student Number_____

Assignment

Choose Physical Distribution, then Distribution Cost Tradeoffs from *The MART's* menus.

1. Your data is shown below. Determine the transportation mode which results in the cheapest total (shipping + carrying) cost for the customer for each item.

Item	Annual Demand	Average Distance	Cost per Unit	Carrying Cost – %	Weight per Unit	Preferred Mode
9 Panel Mirror	700	2,000	146	30	40	_____
Cotton Socks (dozen)	2,100	6,000	48	13	10	_____
Pleated Drapes	2,200	6,000	45	25	12	_____
Nylon Panty (dozen)	1,000	3,100	100	20	2	_____
Kitchen Towels (dozen)	1,900	4,000	54	15	6	_____
Bedspread	1,200	4,000	84	20	16	_____
Carpet Dry Cleaner	410	4,000	245	15	120	_____
21" Stereo TV	180	6,000	400	25	65	_____
3/4 Horsepower Jet Pump	180	6,000	560	20	200	_____
Pet Carrier	3,200	3,500	31	20	8	_____

2. Are there factors other than annual cost that you would want to consider in selecting a transport mode?

_____

_____

3. The program assumes a single mode will be used from the shipping point to the purchaser's receiving dock. Is this appropriate?

_____

_____

AFFILIATED DRY GOODS

54 Gem Foods

Physical distribution was a topic of top management concern for the first time in Gem Foods' 30 year history. Gem is a closely held fruit and vegetable processor. Its products are sold under supermarkets' private labels and Gem's two regional brands.

Physical Distribution Practices

Gem had little warehouse capacity. Produce was, of necessity, packed as it ripened. The product sold under retailers' house brands was shipped immediately to the destination and by the mode specified by the purchaser, usually rail. Gem executives laughingly called this "FOB packing case."

Merchandise packed under Gem's labels was the responsibility of the production manager, Lynn Code, until such time as it was loaded for shipment to a customer. The normal practice was for this executive to engage in large scale contracts for warehouse space at the cheapest rate he could find in the region. This usually resulted in inventory being located in public warehouses in economically depressed areas.

On occasion the cheapest rate would be found in a private warehouse whose owner did not have use for it for a sufficient length of time. Usually these turned out to be in even more depressed areas. Code didn't really care too much for private warehousing. Insurance, any local inventory taxes, and off-loading and reloading the goods were his department's responsibility and frequently turned out to be a nuisance.

The shipping manager, "Carload" Ostermann, was responsible for arranging transportation and minimizing transportation costs. His nickname came from the fact that he would almost never consider a mode other than rail and the cheapest, carload, rates. His response to a salesperson's request for a small or fill-in order for a customer was "let them get their act together and plan ahead."

Ostermann frequently made a fuss over Code's sticking inventory "on the backside of nowhere" and running up transportation costs. Secretly, he didn't mind at all. Over the years he had been successful at getting his department's budget set at a fairly constant percentage of the prior year's transportation costs. Code's warehousing policies, which increased transportation costs, were the foundation of what some referred to as the "Ostermann Empire."

Carload and his rate books were a mystery management didn't understand and would rather ignore. The only basis upon which he was evaluated was a report (monthly and annual) of the tonnage of product shipped and the proportion that did, and did not, move by rail in carload lots.

Forces for Change

The rest of the management team made Lynn and Carload seem downright progressive. However, forces were converging that would permanently disrupt this comfortable little backwater company. The first was in the person of Andrew Gemcroft, scion of the founding family and newly appointed company president. He had recently completed an executive MBA, where he had picked up radical notions, such as product innovation and putting customer needs first. Like any lad (of fifty) he was anxious to make his mark on the firm.

The second force emerged from the company laboratory. A newly hired food technician had failed to understand that his only task was to check for pollutants and contagion and had developed a radical new product. (Some favored letting him go as a disruptive influence.) The new product was a line of jams and jellies which contained very little sugar, yet tasted almost like the real thing.

These jams and jellies were more expensive to produce than the regular product, since sugar is cheaper than fruit, and much more processing was involved. (Gem responded by partially processing the fruit in season, then storing it in bulk until closer to the time when it was needed.) Gem had leased a warehouse near its plant in which to store the in-process and finished good inventory for this line.

The line also had a shorter rated shelf life. The actual shelf life wasn't as much of a problem as retailers' perceptions. They simply had no confidence in the expiration date and insisted on smaller, more frequent orders of fresh-dated product.

The product line had been a huge success in the markets in which it was introduced. Yet, growth was being impeded by the distribution system. A more costly inventory, coupled with customers' desires for more responsive system of filling their orders, had rendered the previous practices obsolete.

Andrew Gemcroft was wholeheartedly behind the new product line, believing the firm should move in the direction of products with a higher value-added. Also, he believed the distribution problems the line was facing were indicative of more general shortcomings in the firm's approach to physical distribution.

Gem had hired a consulting firm specializing in physical distribution to study the problem. The consulting report recommended that Gem adopt the physical distribution concept. It recommended a small simulation, which would let Gem executives try out different courses of action.

Notes

Assignment

Choose Physical Distribution, then the Physical Distribution Simulation from *The MART's* menus. (The variables in the simulation are described in the discussion of the Physical Distribution Program, p. 246)

1.   How would you characterize Gem's physical distribution system?

_____

_____

2.   What could be wrong with using

    a. the lowest cost warehouses?

_____

_____

    b. the cheapest mode of transportation?

_____

_____

3.   Would the problems identified in 2. be more or less severe for the new product line than for Gem's older products?

_____

_____

4. Run the Physical Distribution Simulation. Try to develop the best combination of physical distribution alternatives. Record your choices below.

_____

_____

_____

_____

_____

_____

5. What is the least cost combination yielding a customer service level of 80% of orders filled within 48 hours?

_____

_____

_____

_____

_____

_____

6. What happens to distribution costs as the customer service level is increased?

_____

_____

XI Promotion: Personal Selling

55 Sales Force and Advertising Impact Model: A Description

To plan a budget, a marketer either implicitly, or explicitly assumes that a given change in expenditure will result in a particular change in sales, or profits. The relation between the level of expenditure and the level of sales is called a response function. There are many elements of a marketing mix that can be changed — for example, the quality of the product, price, advertising, promotional support, sales force support, increased distribution, etc. There is a corresponding response function for each of these.

The figures below show two possible response functions. Sometimes the response can be immediate, as in the case of the distribution response function. There may be a threshold level below which there is no response, but once that level is reached there is a substantial response, as in the case with the advertising response curve shown. It is generally assumed that diminished returns set in, once a certain level of expenditure is reached; added expenditure results in little or no sales growth. It is even conceivable that too much expenditure on one element of the mix, say advertising, could, actually, result in a decline in sales.

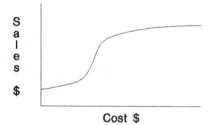

Figure 1 Possible Response Function: Advertising

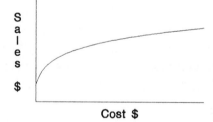

Figure 2 Possible Response Function: Distribution

Usually the marketing manager does not have the resources to make the tests of multiple expenditure levels needed to derive the curve. Instead, they may have bumped up advertising or promotion 20% several quarters ago, and noted a 3% growth in sales. After years of experience observing the ups and downs of their and their competitors' sales, they probably believe they know what would happen to sales if they were to cut their sales force completely, or saturated the market with salespeople.

278

The Model

Single Period

In 1970 A. D. Little developed an equation that would generate a response function — similar to the ones in Figures 1 and 2, with the input of four values. For purposes of this discussion it will be assumed you are considering a change to the sales force budget.

a) *Share after Saturation Sales Force*

This is the maximum market share that would be achieved in one period — usually a quarter — assuming a maximum, or saturation, level of sales force effort.

b) *Share after X% Increase in Sales Force*

This is the increase in sales for a specified percentage increase in expenditure over the previous period. The increase in expenditure chosen will depend on what is reasonable for that product class, and what changes have been made in the past on which the person can base an estimate.

The person then specifies......

c) *Present Market Share*

This is the market share for the reference period. Market share is assumed to remain at this level, given existing expenditures on the various elements of the marketing mix, including the sales force. When using the sales force expenditure model, the existing level of expenditure must be entered.

d) *End of Period Share if No Sales Force*

This is the market share at the end of the period assuming no sales force actively, at all.

Multiple Periods

These four values allow the generation of a one period response function curve. If we want to examine the impact of expenditure changes on several periods, then the long term market share, assuming no more sales force, must be estimated as well. Little's equation then derives a market share decay factor which indicates the effect of expenditure changes in one period on market share in subsequent periods.

To evaluate the profitability of these changes in expenditure, some further inputs are needed. First we need to know the total contribution to overhead and profits that is generated by the present market share. Second, the number of target customers — customers that could be visited by the sales force — need to be estimated since reference sales force expenditures are per target market customer.

The changes to market share and market size — based on an estimate of the growth of the overall market — are used to estimate changes in the contribution to overhead and profit. The expenditure on sales force is then subtracted from this. Several levels of sales force expenditure can be tested and the level found that results in the greatest profits. Alternatively, a target market share may be selected. The model will determine the required sales force expenditure and estimate the resulting profit.

Effectiveness

The amount spent on the sales force does not necessarily reflect the effectiveness of those dollars. Sometimes improvements can be made to the effectiveness of the sales force during their calls. This could be because of improved training, improved hiring practices, or simply because the sales force is gaining experience. Conversely, if the firm suddenly loses many of the senior salespeople, the effectiveness of sales calls may decline.

A second factor that influences the effectiveness of sales force expenditure is the efficiency with which salespeople are able to cover their territory. Improved means of transportation, scheduling, or territory design may improve the sales force's coverage efficiency.

The model handles these two factors by two indices which the manager can adjust. They would normally be set at 1.00 for the reference period, and then changed, say to 1.05, if the manager believes the call effectiveness or coverage efficiency will go up by 5% for a particular period.

Using the Sales Force and Advertising Impact Program

We suggest you load up the program and go to the first screen of either the Sales Force Impact Model, or the Advertising Impact Model.

The allowable range for the *reference expenditures* differs between the sales force and the advertising programs. The sales force program allows anywhere from $1 to $999 per target customer, while the advertising program allows a range from $.01 to $99.99. Market share estimates greater than 100% can only be entered for the saturation and increased levels of spending. Also, the five share estimates *must* be in descending order.

If the period is three months long, then *seasonality indices* may be entered, so that sales figures reflect the quarterly fluctuations. If the period is not a quarter, then these indices should be left at 1.000.

If changes are made to the numbers entered, you should always use <Pg Dn> to leave the screen, so that these changes are incorporated into the analysis. *Note*, you can leave any of the screens at any time, by pressing the <Esc> key.

Enter some values so that you can leave this screen. Once you have seen the response curve graph, you will be able to select the budget testing section of the program.

The budget testing section is designed to allow you to estimate the impact of various budget levels on contribution to overhead and profits. The arrow keys can be used to move about the screen, in order to enter numbers. The reference budget you entered earlier will be shown as the top line budget for each period. This budget is increased twelve times by the amount shown in the increment line, above. Each of these budgets is tested and the resulting contribution shown on the right.

The contribution number highlighted indicates the optimal budget, taking into account the contribution generated during the number of periods you have selected, plus four more. This budget will generally be higher than the budget with the highest contribution shown on the screen, since it takes into account the carry-over effect of the higher budget. If the highlighted line is at the top (bottom) budget, this could mean the optimal budget is more (less) than the one shown on that line. You should test budgets beyond the range shown on the screen.

To change values simply enter the number and move to the next cell using the arrow. Recalculate the contributions by pressing the <Enter> key.

You can increase the range of budget tested by increasing the increment. Doubling the increment will double the range tested. Once an optimal budget is found, you should reduce the increment and enter the highlighted budget level midway down the budget lines. This will allow you to refine your estimate.

Once you have identified a budget level you wish to examine further, highlight a cell on that line and press <Pg Dn>. The program will graph the market shares, then on the next screen it will provide detailed results of market shares and contributions. You might want to press the <Prt Sc> (Print Screen) key at this point in order to preserve your solution.

Make sure you have a printer attached to the computer and that it is turned on and on line, before you press the < Prt Sc > key. Go back and print your parameter input screen as well.

On most systems you should be able to print a copy of the graphs produced by this program. You have to do something before you even start *The MART* program. Enter the word GRAPHICS at a DOS prompt. If the computer cannot find the file then go to the DOS directory, if you are on a hard drive, or insert the DOS disk, and enter GRAPHICS again. If you get no error message, then you know the computer has accepted the command. When you run the Sales Force and Advertising Impact program and wish to create a graph, press the < Prt Sc > key. This will generate an attractive graph that you can analyze and hand in with your assignment, if you like.

56 Great Western State Lottery Corporation(A)

Henri Chaulk has been sales manager at GWS Lottery for 11 years. The last decade had seen rapid growth of lottery sales, paralleled by a proliferation of lottery games. But the tide has turned, and as with many products that have gone before, it appears that lottery games are in the declining stage of the product life cycle. Faced with this possibility, many of GWS's management have been preparing for the worst. General belt-tightening exercises are expected soon, with lay-off notices becoming a major weapon in the fight to maintain profits. Unlike some of the rats who are looking for a safe harbor in which to jump ship, Henri, a believer in DIMBO (Diversity In Marketing Brings Opportunities), sees the situation as an opportunity for marketing, and in his case, the sales force, to save the ship.

GWS Lottery Corp initially sold the State's instant scratch and win game, where a lucky player could spend a dollar and win up to $10,000. Variations on a theme followed, with the price of tickets, the size of the first prize, and the number and size of secondary prizes, all being altered as new games were introduced to appeal to different segments of the market. Then, along came the State's Lottery called Jumbo. Now people could spend a dollar and win up to a million.

Growth Falters

Sales continued to grow as Jumbo's jackpots increased to more than $25 million and new "instants" were introduced every couple of months. However, during the last three years sales had stabilized, and this year, for the first time, sales are down. Players drop old instant games more quickly than before, when new ones are introduced. And when Jumbo's jackpot is down to a couple of million, sales fall more than usual. The peaks are still there for the big jackpots, but the troughs are deeper each time.

In Henri's opinion, there are two main solutions: more push, and more pull. Advertising will provide the pull. He feels advertisements that evoke the pleasure of playing the game will remind and motivate people to play. Ads will, also, provide encouragement for retailers to stock tickets and actively support the games. He believes his sales force to be the main means of pushing.

Chaulk has several tools which he can bring to bear. First, the corporation has recently developed a state of the art marketing information system (MIS) that will provide him with detailed information on the effectiveness of his sales force. Second, he has a Sales Force Impact Program, which will allow him to estimate the impact of changes in sales force efforts on profits. Third, he can experiment with some elements of his sales force to provide reliable input data for the program.

Sales Force and Market Structure

The market is divided into nine territories, each with a district sales manager. Each sales manager supervises the five to eight sales representatives assigned to the district.

Each sales–rep has three types of accounts; the *A accounts* are the larger liquor stores and stores in the 7–11 chain, where management is committed to lottery sales. While they only make up 8% of the possible accounts in a sales–rep's territory, they account for 30% of a rep's visits. The *B accounts* are smaller liquor stores, and other convenience store chains. These stores make up about 20% of a rep's possible accounts, and account for about 50% of the calls. The *C accounts* are the hundreds of independent corner grocery stores and other types of outlets that might sell lottery tickets. They make up 72% of the possible accounts, but the sales–reps devote less than 20% of their visits to these stores.

The sales–rep's main function is to sell packets of tickets — usually two hundred tickets per packet — to the person responsible for a store's purchasing. They explain to the clerks how the games work and instruct them on the security codes. They also deliver posters, advertising, LED signs and other point of sales material.

Growth Opportunities

Build C Accounts

Henri sees two major opportunities for his sales force to improve sales. The first is to expand the accessibility of tickets, thus requiring less effort by potential buyers to purchase tickets and leading to more impulse purchases. Experience has shown that convenient booths in malls boosted sales. There may be many other locations that would provide added convenience to large numbers of players. One recent example occurred when a small store on the ground floor of a large apartment building — a C account — started selling tickets. Within three months, it was selling three times the district's average sales volume per account.

This one experience didn't prove that a concerted effort to sell to C accounts would work, and there could be some cannibalization of existing accounts. On a district wide level, development of these accounts might substantially increase sales. Doing so would, of course, require a larger sales force budget.

Emphasize B Accounts

The second opportunity would be to have sales–reps spend more time with their B accounts, demonstrating to managers that selling lottery tickets could provide more profits to their businesses. The retailers would be shown how to train sales clerks to encourage sales of lottery tickets, and how to utilize the promotional material GWS had specifically designed for the stores. A properly trained sales clerk could increase sales of lottery tickets by 20%, or more. For example, if a customer buys three Jumbo tickets for three dollars, and hands the clerk a five dollar bill, she could ask if they wanted to buy a couple of $1 "instants," as well. Experience showed that half of the time the customer would do so.

Sales Force Experiments

The C Accounts Experiment

Henri conducted experiments in two districts to test his theories. In the Coastal District, he tested the impact of concentrating more selling effort on the C accounts. Five of the sales–reps shifted their efforts from their own territory to an adjacent territory for one day every second week. They concentrated on C accounts. This permitted the measurement of the impact of adding 10% to the sales force in a territory. The MIS was used to accurately assess the nature of the impact and provide measures of repeat purchases by C Accounts, as well as the cost effectiveness of the visits by sales–reps. (What this does not provide is an estimate of what other levels of increased sales force effort would yield, and what the long term effects would be. That is the value of using the Sales Force Impact Program.)

After one quarter, the added effort had resulted in a 3% increase in sales. Henri estimates that if he saturated the marketplace with sales–reps in a particular quarter, targeting C accounts, sales might reach 125% of their base level.

The B Accounts Experiment

A second trial was conducted in the Mount Thom District to test the impact of targeting the B accounts. Five sales–reps spent one day a week in an adjacent territory. This time they focused on maintaining the local rep's A accounts, while the local reps spent more time with their B accounts, training personnel and setting up counter displays. It was found that the 20% increase in sales force expenditure resulted in a 5% increase in sales during the quarter.

If he saturated the marketplace with sales–reps in a particular quarter, concentrating on B accounts, sales might reach 115% of normal.

Henri must choose between the two strategies. He wants to be able to estimate the added contribution to overhead and profits over the next four quarters. Armed with the results of his experiments, he turned to the computer program.

Model Parameters

Chaulk needs to provide several estimates for the program. First, there are a total of 42,000 possible accounts — including A, B and C accounts — in the market, so he enters this number where the program asks for the number of target market customers.

The total quarterly sales force expenditure, including the cost of support staff, travel and telephone expenses, and benefits, is $1,092,000, or $26 per account. Each quarter, after prize money, printing costs and account commissions are paid, there is a contribution of 45 cents per sales dollar to administration and marketing expenses, and profit. Sales of $288,900,000 per average quarter generate $130,000,000 in contribution. Profits are forwarded to the State Government for application to the State's Health and Recreation Department budget.

There is little or no seasonal effect. Sales are down about 5% in the second quarter of the year, but up 5% in the fourth quarter. Market growth, however, is negative, declining at a rate of 1% per quarter, although this is hard to judge, given the large variance in sales from period to period.

Having a virtual monopoly on the market, Henri set the present market share at 100%. If the sales force were cut out altogether in the next quarter, sales would drop to roughly 80% of what they are now, and in the long term, to 50% of present sales.

Henri decides to look at the impact the two options would have on sales over the next year. With trembling hands, he turns to the computer to enter the values.

Assignment

Select Promotion: Budgeting from *The MART's* menu and complete the following exercises.

1. Input values for targeting each type of account, determine the optimal sales force budget for each strategy and fill in the table below.

		C Accounts	B Accounts
Optimal budget per quarter		_____	_____
Market shares in	P1	_____	_____
	P2	_____	_____
	P3	_____	_____
	P4	_____	_____
Contribution to profits after sales force	P1	_____	_____
	P2	_____	_____
	P3	_____	_____
	P4	_____	_____
Total contribution after sales force, over 4 quarters		_____	_____
Required investment in sales force over 4 quarters		_____	_____

Which accounts would you target and why?

_____

_____

_____

_____

GWS LOTTERY CORP.(A)

2. When experiments are conducted with employees, they often perform better than they would under normal conditions. What would be the optimal budget if a 10% increase in efforts aimed at C accounts was most likely to result in a 2% increase in sales, and a 20% increase in sales effort aimed at B accounts produced a 3% increase in sales? Is the difference in estimates sufficient to warrant caution when establishing the budget?

_____

_____

_____

_____

_____

_____

_____

3. Henri feels he may not receive approval of the optimal sales force budget. He feels he may receive support for an increased budget, if he can demonstrate that he can expect to halt the decline in sales over the next four periods (sales in period 4 would be 105% of period 0 due to seasonality). Should the same types of accounts be targeted? How much will he have to increase his budget?

_____

_____

_____

_____

_____

4. Is it reasonable to try and reverse declining sales in this market by increasing the sales force budget, rather than spending the money to develop new improved games?

_____

_____

_____

_____

_____

_____

_____

5. Emphasizing the B and C accounts will have an impact on the relative coverage efficiencies. If B accounts are targeted more heavily, the coverage efficiency should improve by 2%, since they are more numerous than A accounts, resulting in reduced travel time between stores. If C accounts are targeted, the coverage efficiency will improve by 4%, because they are more numerous still. How does this affect the selection of target market and the optimal sales force budget?

_____

_____

_____

_____

_____

_____

6. Henri is considering the use of telemarketing in order to improve the call effectiveness of his sales force. A team of inside salespeople would telephone prospective accounts in order to determine their interest in selling lottery tickets. Only those prospects expressing interest would be visited by a salesperson. The telemarketing team could also handle ticket reordering, and solve many of the problems accounts may have. The result would be that the sales force would be able to spend much more of their time selling and training, thus improving their call effectiveness by 40%. The added cost would be about $250,000 per quarter.

a. Is it better to invest the money in a 25% sales force increase, or to spend it on telemarketing? (*Hint*: to see the impact of a 25% sales force budget increase, set the budget increment to .25, leave the call effectiveness index at 1.00 and use the results of the second budget line.)

_____

_____

_____

_____

_____

_____

b. After subtracting the extra million dollars from revenue, is the contribution after four periods greater with telemarketing or without it? How much extra contribution, if any, did the telemarketing generate?

_____

_____

_____

_____

_____

_____

57 Hifax Warrantee Inc.

Judy Lowe, V.P. Marketing of Hifax Warranties Inc., calmly listened to her sales manager, Ralph Costain, as he forcefully tried to make his point.

"In this business success depends on the effectiveness of our sales force. Cut back the frequency of visits to customers, and we'll see our sales evaporate faster than you can imagine. I think we would benefit from an increase in our budget. I also believe this training program you are considering is a waste of time and, as for that scheduling program you bought, throw it away!"

"Ralph," she said, "you've been running that sales force by the seat of your pants for so long they've about worn through. We are losing market share and I'm not going to put money into something based on your gut feel anymore. I intend to thoroughly analyze the cost effectiveness of the sales force and come up with a more rational means of allocating the budget."

The Warrantee Industry

Hifax is the sixth largest warrantee company in a multi-billion dollar a year business. When consumers buy an appliance, such as a microwave oven, it generally comes with either a ninety day, or one year warrantee. They have, however, the option of buying an extended warrantee for another year or two, for between $30 and $100. Not everybody buys an extended warrantee, but about 60% do.

The retailer sells these warranties as an added feature to the appliance, keeping roughly 45% of the revenue, the remainder going to the warrantee company. The consumers are not given a choice of warranties, but the retailer would like to have as attractive a warrantee as possible, as this can be a very profitable part of the business. The consumers know little about the companies behind the warranties, or what the options are in the various warranties on the market. The retailers are, therefore, free to switch warrantee suppliers whenever it suits them, and are frequently persuaded to do so by warrantee salespeople. As Ralph noted, the sales force plays an important role in gaining and maintaining market share.

The Situation

It turned out that there was little information except Ralph's gut feel on which to base any decisions. Fortunately a sales force budgeting program was available that would take Ralph's estimates and transform them into a sales response curve which could be used for estimating the impact of changes to the sales force budget, coverage efficiency and call effectiveness. The table below provides his estimates.

Table 17   Ralph's Estimates

Number of periods to be tested	4
Reference sales force expenditure	$100
Share after saturation sales force	8.00%
An increase of 20% in the sales force budget was used as the bench mark.	
Share after **20%** increase in sales force	7.68%
Present market share	7.50%
End of quarter share if no sales force	6.50%
Eventual share if sales force cut out	2.00%
Reference quarterly contribution	$15,000,000
Seasonality sales indices	Q1 **0.400**
	Q2 1.000
	Q3 1.000
	Q4 **1.600**
Quarterly growth in industry sales	-1.00%
Number of target market customers	22,500

Assignment

Select Promotion: Budgeting from *The MART's* menu and complete the following exercises.

1. Input the figures in Table 17 and examine the resulting sales response curve. Does the shape of the curve make sense? Is there more to be lost by reducing the budget than there is to be gained from increasing it? What is the maximum you might spend on the sales force per target market customer and still gain market share?

    _____

    _____

    _____

2. Based on Ralph's estimates should the sales force budget be changed?

    Present contribution after sales force   _____

    Optimal sales force budget   _____

    Contribution after sales force at optimal
    sales force budget   _____

    _____

    _____

3. Judy has a sales force scheduling program that will improve coverage efficiency by 8% (enter an index of 1.08 for each period). Aside from the cost of the program, she will have to purchase personal computers for each member of the sales force. Is this a better option than adding the $6 per target customer — the equivalent of hiring 5 to 6 more sales people — to the base sales force budget? (Assume a base budget of $100.)

    Contribution after sales force
    if scheduling program implemented _____

    Contribution after sales force
    if $6 is added to the base budget   _____

    _____

        HIFAX WARANTEE INC.

4. Judy can send her sales force to a Sales Effectiveness course that should increase their call effectiveness by 10%. Half the sales force would be away for two weeks in the first quarter of the year, half in the second. This would reduce the call efficiency for those two quarters to .93, until all of the sales people have taken the course. Half will have completed the course by the end of the first quarter giving a 5% boost to call effectiveness in the second quarter. By the third quarter when everyone will have completed the course, call efficiency will return to 100% and call effectiveness will rise to 110%. It should continue at that level for at least another 3 quarters.

Will the course pay for itself over the first four quarters? Will it pay for itself over the first six quarters? (Assume she is starting with a $100 budget.)

	Four Quarters	Six Quarters
Contribution after sales force, no course	_____	_____
Contribution after sales force, course taken	_____	_____
Less the cost of the course	_____	_____
Gain or loss of contribution after sales force	_____	_____

_____

_____

5. Judy wants to achieve an 8.8% market share by the fourth quarter. How much will she have to spend on each target customer in order to achieve her goal? What will it cost her in terms of lost contribution after sales force?

Sales force budget required _____

Lost contribution after sales force _____

XII Promotion: Advertising

58 Great Western State Lottery Corporation(B)

The Great Western State Lottery Corporation is facing declining markets. The last decade saw rapid growth of lottery sales, accompanied by a proliferation of lottery games. But the tide has turned, and like many products before, it appears that lottery games are in the declining stage of the product life cycle.

GWS Lottery Corp initially introduced the State's instant scratch and win game, where a lucky player could spend a dollar and win up to $10,000. Variations on a theme followed, with the price of tickets, the size of the first prize, and the number and size of secondary prizes, all being altered as new games were introduced to appeal to different segments of the market. Then GWS introduced the State's Lottery called Jumbo. Now people could spend a dollar and win up to a million dollars.

Sales continued to grow as Jumbo's jackpots increased to more than $25 million and new "instants" were introduced every couple of months. However, for the last three years sales had stabilized, and this year, for the first time, sales are down. Players are quicker to drop old instant games when new ones are introduced. And when Jumbo's jackpot is down to a couple of million, sales fall more than usual. The peaks are still there for the big jackpots, but the troughs are deeper each time.

Advertising

Karen Drake, advertising manager, would like to think that increased advertising would profitably halt the sales decline. She is, however, the first to admit that she has a biased point of view. She has decided to ignore this and let others present counter-arguments if they can, while she makes a logical and forceful case for increased spending on advertising.

Karen feels she has reasonable grounds on which to base her arguments. Up to now, GWS has only advertised specific games such as Jumbo, special draw games and the instant scratch games introduced every three months. All of these ads featured a single game, but none of them promote the playing of lottery games, in general. Karen believes that many people, particularly those who had stopped playing recently, are not interested in messages about games with which they are already familiar. They may simply no longer view lottery games as an option, when they consider entertainment alternatives, or gifts. Maybe the dreamers have lost the dream and no longer see the benefits of buying tickets.

Current Spending. Drake classifies lottery games as a consumer impulse, or convenience good. Other companies selling low cost consumer products spend much more of their revenue on advertising. (Admittedly they tend to be in more competitive markets which justify higher advertising expenditures.) One listing of major consumer package goods companies showed their advertising expenditures ranging from 1.5% of sales, to 31.4%, with an average of 6.9%. GWS spends about 1.3% of its revenue on advertising, which suggests to Karen that they could substantially increase their budget and not be too far out of line.

Justification

There are two major reasons for the relatively low level of expenditure. First, the lottery's board of directors is made up of Government officials who feel that the State should receive at least 47% of the State lottery's revenue. Some board members disagree with the argument that total sales would increase to such a degree that the State's dollar profit would be greater, if some of this 47% were put toward marketing or prizes. Others point out that the ticket buyer expects most of the money to go to the State. This means that increases in administrative costs, such as marketing, are resisted by the board.

The second reason is that many people consider lottery-playing a sin. Too much advertising of lotteries might create a backlash, which would more than offset any benefits gained from increased advertising. The problem is, it is difficult to predict what

Table 18 Karen's Estimates for the Advertising Impact Program

Number of periods to be tested		4
Reference expenditure on advertising		0.84
Share after saturation advertising		110.00%
Share after **20%** increase in advertising		103.00%
Present market share		100.00%
End of quarter share if no advertising		95.00%
Eventual share if no advertising		70.00%
Reference company contribution		$130,000,000
Seasonality sales indices	Q1	1.000
	Q2	0.950
	Q3	1.000
	Q4	1.050
Period growth in industry sales		-1.00%
Number of target market customers		2,400,000

amount of advertising will create this backlash.

Computer Inputs

The current advertising budget is $2,016,000 per quarter, targeted at the 2.4 million players in the state. Being as honest with herself as possible, Karen made the estimates shown in Table 18 and entered them into the Advertising Impact Program. GWS has a monopoly on lotteries in the state, so she set the standard market share to 100%.

As these estimates produced very supportive results, she went to the quarterly planning session with senior management loaded for bear. After she presented her findings, there ensued, not unexpectedly, considerable debate as to the validity of Karen's assumptions and the impact of these assumptions on the analysis. These senior people felt that their years of experience would enable them to make better estimates and, based on past futile arguments, Karen was prepared to agree with them.

She distributed a form to each of those present and asked them to fill in the blanks with their best guesses for the values required. (See Table 19.) She then propped her portable computer on the conference table and proceeded to enter each of these guesses to see what the estimated impact of increased advertising would be. This was a calculated risk, but she hoped that, even using the skeptics' estimates, the results would support her request for an increased advertising budget.

Table 19 Senior Managers' Estimates of Market Response to Advertising

			Individual		
	A	B	C	D	E
Share after saturation advertising	120	105	110	140	110
Share after 20% increase in advertising	105	101	103	110	102
Present market share	100	100	100	100	100
End of period share if no advertising	90	97	80	95	95
Eventual share if no advertising	40	90	40	90	70

Assignment

Select Promotion: Budgeting from *The MART's* menu and complete the following exercises.

1. Examine the response curve generated by Karen's estimates. Pick a budget level you feel will optimize the cost effectiveness of advertising. What is the advertising budget per target customer? What is the added advertising budget (in millions)? Use the budget testing section of the program to determine how much "contribution less advertising" your new budget should generate. How much is the added contribution? Does it look like an increase in advertising would pay off?

Original Budget $.84   Original Contribution $499M

New Budget (per cust.)_____   New Contribution _____

Added Budget (total) _____   Added Contribution _____

_____

_____

2. What is the optimal advertising budget derived by the program using Karen's estimates? Calculate the added advertising budget and the resulting added contribution after advertising. Would you say that the added contribution less advertising you derived in question one is close to the optimal derived from the model?

Original Budget $.84   Original Contribution $499M

New Budget (per cust.)_____   New Contribution _____

Added Budget (total) _____   Added Contribution _____

_____

_____

3. What are the optimal budgets given the estimates of the others?

    A. Budget $_____   Contribution $_____

    B. Budget $_____   Contribution $_____

    C. Budget $_____   Contribution $_____

    D. Budget $_____   Contribution $_____

    E. Budget $_____   Contribution $_____

4. Would you recommend that GWS change its advertising level? If so, what would you change it to and why?

    _____

    _____

    _____

    _____

    _____

    _____

    _____

    _____

5. John Borden, the research manager, reminded everybody that he had been carrying out experiments on advertising copy, using the new CACTUS service (Computer Assisted Copy Testing User System). The system requires a group of up to forty people to watch commercials. While they watch the commercial they continually record their reaction to the ad by turning a dial on a handset. Early results indicated that GWS would be able to upgrade the average quality of their advertising copy by 15%. He felt that this might be sufficient to reverse the decline in sales.

    Karen agreed that it might help, but suggested that John use a more conservative estimate of the improved copy effectiveness, say about 8% (the copy effectiveness indices would be set to 1.08). The CACTUS service would add about 2% to the advertising budget ($161,000 over four quarters). This would have to be subtracted from the contribution less advertising.

Is investment in the CACTUS service worthwhile? How does it affect the value of contribution less advertising, if the advertising budget is kept the same?

Original Contribution less Advertising $499,138,208

Contribution less Advertising with CACTUS $_____

Subtract the cost of CACTUS $_____

Gain or loss in contribution with CACTUS $_____

Is it better to put the money into the advertising budget directly (set the test increment to .02 and use the second budget line)?

_____

_____

_____

6. How confident can you be in these results? How sensitive are the results to changes in the estimates? (A common approach for measuring the sensitivity of results is to vary the values by 10% and examine the impact of the change on the model's output. In this case, the estimates are anchored to the standard, or present, market share and we use a plus or minus 10% around the change in market share predicted.) Karen predicted the market share would increase to 103% with a 20% increase in advertising, up 3% over the present share. To measure the sensitivity of the results to her estimate we decrease it by 10% to 2.7% and increase it by 10% to 3.3%, giving us market shares of 102.7% and 103.3% to test.

Determine the outputs associated with the 10% changes to Karen's estimates listed below. Remember to reset the variables back to their original value before testing the next variable. Graph the four lines on the graph below. To which of the estimates is the optimal advertising budget most sensitive? How confident would you be in the predictions of this model?

Market share after saturation advertising

Market Share Estimate	Optimal Ad Budget
109.00%	_____
110.00%	_____
111.00%	_____

Market share after 20% increase in advertising

Market Share Estimate	Optimal Ad Budget
102.70%	_____
103.00%	_____
103.30%	_____

Market share after one year if advertising is stopped

Market Share Estimate	Optimal Ad Budget
94.50%	_____
95.00%	_____
95.50%	_____

Market share over long run if advertising is stopped

Market Share Estimate	Optimal Ad Budget
67.00%	_____
70.00%	_____
73.00%	_____

Sensitivity Graph

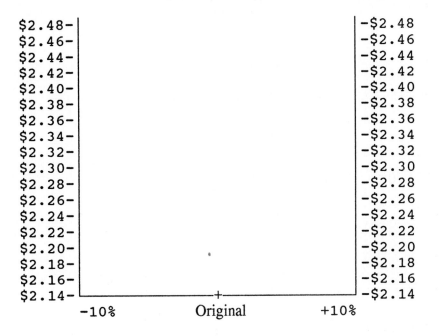

```
$2.48-                                    -$2.48
$2.46-                                    -$2.46
$2.44-                                    -$2.44
$2.42-                                    -$2.42
$2.40-                                    -$2.40
$2.38-                                    -$2.38
$2.36-                                    -$2.36
$2.34-                                    -$2.34
$2.32-                                    -$2.32
$2.30-                                    -$2.30
$2.28-                                    -$2.28
$2.26-                                    -$2.26
$2.24-                                    -$2.24
$2.22-                                    -$2.22
$2.20-                                    -$2.20
$2.18-                                    -$2.18
$2.16-                                    -$2.16
$2.14-                                    -$2.14
      -10%        Original        +10%
```

To which estimate is the optimal advertising budget output most sensitive? How confident would you be in the predictions of this model?

_____

_____

_____

_____

_____

_____

59 Merlin Foods Limited [1]

With two weeks under her belt in her new job as Director of Marketing, Children's Products Division at Merlin Foods, Limited, Jane McLean contemplated the stable but lackluster performance of the six brands of children's pasta she had just inherited. Her boss, Frank Stevens, V. P. Children's Products, was an affable man, but expected a lot from her. He had said to Jane after their first meeting, "You come highly recommended, Jane. I know you will find a way to light a fire under this business and deliver those healthy profits the company wants."

Sensing that familiar surge of excitement and pressure when faced with a challenge, Jane thought of the conversation with Helen Sachs, her counterpart at the advertising agency that handled all of Merlin Foods' advertising. If Merlin Foods was going to advertise next year, the agency's media department needed an annual budget figure by September 1, two weeks away. September was always a busy month for media buyers, especially children's television buyers, because there was so much demand from advertisers like Merlin Foods and so little inventory.

Her conversation with Helen that morning echoed in her head. "Helen, I've been here two weeks. I've barely had time to size up the business, and to keep all the brand names and their respective shares straight, let alone to figure out what we should be spending on advertising next year. I can't just take last year's number and increase it by forty percent. I want to be able to assess what impact advertising in the past has had on our business. Before you know it, we'll be committed to a whopping increase, and I won't be able to justify it to my senior management."

Despite three new product launches in the past five years and healthy advertising expenditures in 1985, 1988 and 1989 (Table 20), her three new brands had grown a paltry 1.9 share points, while Merlin's total share points had only increased 1.4 share points since 1984. Meanwhile, the #1 player in the market, Deli Fine Foods, had managed to grow 3.3 share points over the same period, even though they hadn't done as well with their new product launches. Jane had to admit that Deli's 60% increase in advertising spending in 1987 must have helped. She had a suspicion, but couldn't prove it, that despite her company's growing advertising expenditure, not enough funds were being spent on the two core brands in her portfolio, Lotsa-Letters and Critter-getti. A lot of the increases in advertising were going to the new products.

---

[1]This case was co-authored with Martha Reynolds.

Just then the telephone rang. It was Helen. "Jane, we are in business. I've just spent the last half hour with the media guys and gals. They gave me a new computer program that will help us analyze your situation quickly and give us a good feel for the budget figure we need. I'll be over in thirty minutes."

Company Background

Merlin Foods Ltd. pioneered the development of children's pasta products back in 1965 with the introduction of Lotsa–Letters. Its flagship brand, Merlin's Spaghetti, introduced in the fifties, has been dying the inevitable death of a generic, undifferentiated brand. There are five other canned spaghetti products on the market. When a competitor followed Merlin's lead and launched its own version of a shaped pasta for children in the mid-seventies, the battle-ground was joined. Merlin responded by launching its second shaped product, Critter–getti. Merlin's two major competitors each introduced two brands in the years preceding 1984.

Since 1984, Merlin has taken a more aggressive stance by launching three additional shaped pasta products: Freddy Bears — based on a popular children's cartoon — in 1984, Circles and Squares in early 1988, and Monster-getti late the same year. The introduction of these brands has been supported by substantial advertising dollars, some new, some shifted from existing brands.

Market Background

Canned pasta is a three quarter billion dollar (wholesale) market. Volume growth has been steady during the last five years, a function of conflicting trends. There has been a shift away from canned goods, toward fresh, non-processed food by those looking for a healthier diet. (Canned goods are seen as containing additives and preservatives, although canned pasta has not been affected to the same extent as other canned goods.) Counteracting this trend has been the increase in families with both parents working, and in single parent families. As a result, parents have less time to prepare meals for their children. Canned pasta products are seen as a convenient and reasonably nutritious meal. The introduction of seven new brands supported by advertising has given market growth added momentum.

It is estimated that there are roughly 13 million homes with children between 1 and 13 years of age. While the parents are the purchaser — sometimes the consumer — of the product, the children are assumed to choose the brand. The earlier canned pasta products (spaghetti and ravioli) appealing to the whole family account for about 50% of sales volume, while the newer brands, focusing entirely on children, account for the remainder.

Three companies, each marketing a portfolio of brands, account for close to 90% of sales volume. (See Table 20.) Consumers are extremely price sensitive. Consequently, most brands are priced within 5%–10% of each other. Although a good deal of feature pricing and display activity still takes place at the retail level, manufacturers have attempted to create "added value" for consumers through innovative promotions, such as can-label offers and special in-store events.

Table 20 Company and Market Data

	1984	1985	1986	1987	1988	1989
MARKET SHARES						
Merlin Foods	30.0%	32.4%	32.9%	31.1%	31.9%	31.4%
Lotsa–Letters	13.0%	12.5%	12.4%	12.0%	12.1%	11.4%
Critter–getti	9.0%	9.1%	9.4%	8.9%	8.5%	7.7%
Freddy Bears	0.6%	4.0%	4.5%	4.2%	3.8%	3.4%
Spaghetti	7.4%	6.8%	6.6%	6.0%	5.0%	4.1%
Circles & Squares	—	—	—	—	2.0%	2.6%
Monster–getti	—	—	—	—	0.5%	2.2%
Deli Fine Foods	34.0%	35.2%	35.9%	36.6%	37.2%	37.3%
Highlander	22.0%	23.5%	21.8%	22.0%	20.3%	21.0%
All Other Brands	15.0%	9.4%	9.4%	10.3%	10.0%	10.3%
MERLIN'S ADVERTISING EXPENDITURES (000)	$600	$800	$710	$800	$1,000	$1,200
MARKET GROWTH	1%	4%	1%	2%	3%	4%

The exact impact of advertising has never been accurately determined, but it is known to be critical for at least two reasons. First, there is a continual turnover of consumers, as children enter the market at age 2 and leave at age 13. Each year the producers must bring their brands to the attention of a new crop of consumers. Without this continuing advertising a brand's sales would quickly fad away. A second critical factor is advertising's role in maintaining dealer support. If the brands with smaller market shares are not advertised, dealers will start pulling them off the shelves.

Setting the advertising budget is an annual event, since television space is purchased on a 52 week basis. Traditionally, Merlin buys 52 weeks of advertising on children's time programs — Saturday and Sunday morning, weekday lunch (12:00–1:30 p.m). and after school (4:00–6:00 p.m.). Its five advertised brands are rotated through in blocks of three to six weeks (spaghetti is not advertised). Although the one year time frame reduces their flexibility in reacting to competitors' strategies, it is considerably more cost efficient than buying spot TV.

The Analysis

Jane and Helen sit down at the computer, boot up the Advertising Impact Model program and examine the screen. The program asks for a series of inputs, some of which are easy to provide, others are not. First, it asks for an estimate of the advertising budget required to maintain sales at a standard level. This is not a number that is easy to estimate. Sales vary up to two market share points a year, as a result of several factors. One important factor is, obviously, manufacturers' marketing efforts, the major influence being the introduction of new brands. For example, in late 1984 Freddy Bears was introduced; by 1985 sales of this brand had grown dramatically. Half of the sales were cannibalized from other Merlin brands, while the other half, worth two share points, were new business. Sales in 1988 and 1989 had also increased, due, in part, to the introduction of two more new brands.

Market growth has been one or two percent per year, except for those years when new products were introduced (1985, 1988 and 1989), when the market grew at 3% or 4%. When the market is growing, the firms tend to spend more on advertising in order to capture the growth segment of the market. This means that, in order to maintain market share in those years, Merlin had to spend substantially more. Of course, if they want to *gain* share points they have to spend even more, again. Looking at the share figures in Table 20, Jane feels that any gains in the last four years by Merlin have been because of the introduction of new brands, and that its market share would actually have declined, if she subtracted the growth due to new brands.

The competition has not introduced any new brands since 1984. They have increased their advertising budgets, instead. Deli Foods raised their expenditure 60% in 1987, alone. Merlin countered with an increase of 25% in 1988 and 20% in 1989. However, most of their added spending went for the new brands. Jane feels that, in the absence of new brand introductions, Merlin will have to spend more heavily just to hold onto market share. She believes that a budget of $5 million will maintain market share in a no-growth state, but another $2 million will be needed for every percentage point of market growth. Since the market is forecast to grow 2% next year (assuming no new brand introductions), this suggests a budget of $9 million, or $.69 per household for the 13 million households in the market.

She then has to estimate the impact of advertising budgets on market share. Since market shares never fluctuated more than two percent, even when there have been substantial increases in advertising, she feels the most Merlin's share could grow to would be 35.5% next year, even if they spend ten times as much. She feels that a 50% increase in advertising over the standard level would yield a 32.4% market share. She sets the standard market share at the 1989 level, 31.4%. It isn't hard to calculate what will happen to share if advertising were dropped altogether. Dealers will start to pull the brands from their shelves. The result will be a decline to 24% by the end of the year. In the long run sales will drop to a low of 13% if advertising is cut altogether.

Total contributions from these brands has been close to $67 million (before advertising and promotion). The industry is forecast to grow at 2% and there are 13 million households in the target market.

Section_____   Name_____

                                     Student Number_____

Assignment

Select Promotion: Budgeting from *The MART's* menu and complete the following exercises.

1. Look at the response function resulting from Jane's estimates. What are its characteristics? Does it seem reasonable to you? Why?

    _____

    _____

    _____

    _____

    _____

2. What is the optimal budget for next year?

    $_____

3. What are the alternative methods of setting advertising budgets? Which ones can this program assist in evaluating? How would the program be applied?

    _____

    _____

    _____

    _____

    _____

    _____

    _____

MERLIN FOODS LIMITED

4.   How confident can you be in these results?   How sensitive are the results to changes in the estimates? (A common approach for measuring the sensitivity of results is to vary the values by 10% and examine the impact of the change on the model's output. In this case, the estimates are anchored to the standard, or present, market share and we use a plus or minus 10% around the change in market share predicted.) Jane predicted that market share would increase to 32.4% with a 50% increase in advertising, up 1% over the present share.   To measure the sensitivity of the results to her estimate, we decrease it by 10% to 0.9% and increase it by 10% to 1.1%, giving us market shares of 32.3% and 32.5% to test.

Determine the outputs associated with the 10% changes to the inputs listed below. Remember to reset the variables to their original values before testing the next variable. Graph the four lines on the graph below.

Market share after saturation advertising

Market Share Estimate	Optimal Ad Budget
35.09%	_____
35.50%	_____
35.91%	_____

Market share after 50% increase in advertising

Market Share Estimate	Optimal Ad Budget
32.30%	_____
32.40%	_____
32.50%	_____

Market share after one year if advertising is stopped

Market Share Estimate	Optimal Ad Budget
23.16%	_____
24.00%	_____
24.84%	_____

Market share over long run if advertising is stopped

Market Share Estimate	Optimal Ad Budget
11.06%	_____
13.00%	_____
14.94%	_____

Sensitivity Graph

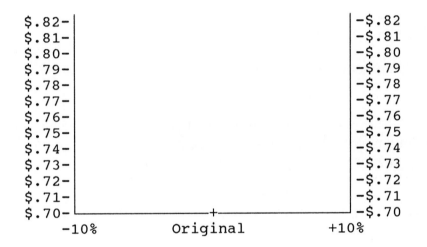

```
$.82-|                                    |-$.82
$.81-|                                    |-$.81
$.80-|                                    |-$.80
$.79-|                                    |-$.79
$.78-|                                    |-$.78
$.77-|                                    |-$.77
$.76-|                                    |-$.76
$.75-|                                    |-$.75
$.74-|                                    |-$.74
$.73-|                                    |-$.73
$.72-|                                    |-$.72
$.71-|                                    |-$.71
$.70-|_____+_____|-$.70
       -10%           Original         +10%
```

To which estimate is the optimal advertising budget output most sensitive?   How confident would you be in the predictions of this model?

_____

_____

_____

_____

_____

5. Jane is also considering a switch to a new advertising agency that promises to improve the cost efficiency of their advertising. The agency has purchased the rights to several syndicated children's programs. These programs are then sold to television stations at a much reduced price in return for half of the advertising spots in the show. The agency then turns around and sells these spots at a greatly discounted rate to its clients. They claim that this system reduces the price of advertising by a fifth, making the advertising dollar go twenty-five percent further.

    If these numbers are correct, what will Jane's advertising budget be, and how much money will she save, if she decides to maintain market share at 31.4%?

    Advertising Budget _____ Saving _____

    What would be her gain in market share and contribution after advertising, if she keeps her budget the same?

    Gain in Market Share _____ %

    Gain in Contribution $_____

6. Jane feels that too much emphasis has been put on the new brands, and that the slide in sales of the older brands could be turned around, if they were promoted. She feels a campaign aimed jointly at parents and children promoting joint consumption, and emphasizing that adults can enjoy the taste of canned spaghetti products, would be much more effective copy than the children-only ads they produce now. If these ads improved copy effectiveness by 10%, what would be the impact on market share and contribution after advertising next year?

    _____

    _____

    _____

    _____

    _____

    _____

7. The strategy of introducing new brands seems to be working. Why would Jane consider putting more emphasis on advertising instead?

_____

_____

_____

_____

_____

_____

8. What would you recommend Jane do?

_____

_____

_____

_____

_____

_____

MERLIN FOODS LIMITED

60 Media Strategy: Advertising Reach and Frequency.

Advertising is a topic on which we can all agree; it's something we love to hate. It also seems to be something we love to talk about. The subject of these conversations is the ads themselves, the expression of the creative strategy. Equally important, but less visible (and less likely to be discussed at coffee break) is the advertiser's media strategy: the selection of the medium or media in which the advertisement will be run.

Developing a media strategy involves a complex matching of various characteristics of the product, the target market, the message and the specific ad, to the available media and their audiences. Having determined the media to be used, say newspaper and magazines, one must still select media vehicles, perhaps *Time* and *The Wall Street Journal*, and set a schedule when the ads will be run.

These are important decisions and the complexity of the full process is beyond the scope of this book. Advertising agencies have large media departments, staffed by specialists supported by computers and complex models, to accomplish these tasks. The exercises here are designed to give you a brief, and much reduced, introduction to this aspect of marketing management.

The Reach and Frequency Model

We will discuss the Reach and Frequency program before introducing the individual cases. When using this model, your task is to allocate an advertising budget among six media which vary widely in cost, circulation and their success at reaching your target market. Your objective is to develop a media plan which will accomplish your advertising objectives as economically as possible.

Initial data describing the population, target market and media are stored for each case. You will have the opportunity to change these parameters, to see how sensitive your solution is to the model's assumptions.

317

Output

As measures of your success we will focus, primarily, on two frequently used indicators of the effectiveness of a media plan: reach and frequency of exposure. Exposure will be defined as bringing the ad to a member of the audience, so that there is a chance for the senses to be activated. The *reach* of an advertisement is the number who are exposed at least once. *Frequency* is the number of exposures received by those who are exposed. Within a fixed budget there is a tradeoff between reach and frequency.

Media Overlap. In determining reach, the model considers overlap, the fact that the same person may be reached by several media. That person is only counted once in estimating reach. In determining frequency all exposures contribute equally to the total.

Impact Score. In addition to reach and frequency, we have provided an impact score. This is a complex function of reach and frequency, weighted by your judgment as to the impact of a particular medium. If you feel that television will have greater influence than newspaper in a given situation, then a given reach and frequency achieved using TV will have a higher impact score than if it were the result of newspaper ads.

Model Assumptions

The model allows for the fact that the number exposed may differ to a greater or lesser degree from the rated circulation, or audience. We all know that the water pressure drops during commercials, because program viewers have left the room to make use of other facilities. With the profusion of remote controls, zapping commercials is a common practice. Alternatively, a magazine featuring product ratings may be heavily consulted in libraries, thus having the potential for achieving exposures far in excess of its circulation.

Target Market Focus. The program assumes that the organization's only interest, in the campaign with which you will be concerned, is in communicating with its target market. Exposures to those not in the target market are of no interest, or even seen as a disadvantage. This is realistic. Take an ad for a feminine hygiene product in the local newspaper. Approximately 50% of the circulation the advertiser pays for is not, never was and never will be purchasers of the product. Or consider a tourism campaign. The themes that may be used to attract travelers (quaint, rustic, old fashioned) may be positively offensive, if viewed by the local residents depicted in the advertising.

The reach and frequency model considers the percent of those exposed by a media vehicle, that are in your target market. An alternative with a high cost may be quite economical, if a large proportion of those exposed are members of your target market.

This focus on the target market is reflected in the summary statistics presented for your media strategy. Gross reach and frequency measures are shown for both the target market and the total population, as an indication of what portion of your advertising effort is reaching its target. Final measures are only displayed for the target market.

Effective Exposure. At some point, any advertisement may be subject to wear out effects; more exposures will not have a further impact. To incorporate this effect, the model uses the concept of an effective exposure. This is defined as an exposure to the target market that does not cause the average frequency to exceed the identified wear out point. Thus, you may find that you have achieved a large number of exposures to your target market and, yet, have a relatively small number of effective exposures because the same individuals are being repeatedly exposed.

Each medium used is considered to be a unique campaign and subject to its own wear out point. Thus, if you achieve a frequency of 18 using newspaper, your effective exposures may only be eight or ten. If you achieved half of the 18 with newspaper ads and half with TV, your effective exposures could be 18.

Media Costs. Cost per thousand (CPM), which is commonly used for describing and comparing the costs of media with different sized audiences, is incorporated into the model. CPM – Effective is used as a measure for comparing the cost of achieving *effective* exposures to the target market.

Features

The simulation is completely menu guided. Several factors should be noted. First, when you begin the program you will have a choice between seeing graphic displays and going directly to a tabular presentation. The former visually demonstrates the impact of the values being used and should be chosen at least the first time the program is run. The tabular presentation is quicker, but less informative. In either instance, you may change the value of any variable.

The second feature to which you should be alerted is the meaning of values displayed on magenta backgrounds. These are the results of calculations, or values carried forward from a previous screen. They are, for the moment, fixed and can only be changed by going back and changing the parameters used in the calculation.

Finally, when entering budgets for the various media, the program will not give fractional insertions. Say you enter $20,000 for advertising in the local newspaper and the cost per insertion is $6,000. The program will show three insertions and increment the total budget figure by $18,000. The $20,000 you budgeted will not be changed, but all calculations will be based on spending $18,000 for newspaper advertising.

61 REFORM

Fairfield is a medium sized industrial city in the rust belt. It went through some hard times in the late seventies and early eighties. For example, a major employer that supplied hydraulic valves and pumps used in industrial and construction equipment, was particularly hard hit, when its customers lost world market share to foreign competitors.

In response, Fairfield diversified its economy. Consolidated Valve and other firms undertook major corporate restructurings, all of which were painful processes. As a result, Fairfield and its employers were well positioned to prosper from the resurgence of industrial demand in the late eighties.

From Movement to Party

REFORM is Fairfield's political nonparty. It began as a bipartisan, apolitical, volunteer organization devoted to attracting new businesses. When REFORM found the ward healer politics of the old machine impeding these efforts, it started lending its support to selected candidates put forth by one of the two major parties. Those chosen were believed to be supportive of REFORM's efforts.

It was a short step to putting forth REFORM candidates. Though it still titled itself a movement, it was, in fact, a third party in municipal politics. In the last election, REFORM received 45% of the popular vote, though that translated into only a third of the council seats, due to the concentration of its supporters in the upscale neighborhoods and suburbs.

The Campaign

The coming election was shaping up as a single issue campaign, the issue being mandatory recycling of solid waste. Like cities throughout North America, Fairfield's landfill was reaching capacity and would have to be closed within a few years. Also typically, the NIMBY (Not In My Back Yard) syndrome impeded the search for a new site.

REFORM had long advocated recycling and now saw it as an issue whose time had come. Polls indicated growing public support. Since REFORM had the territory staked out, the other parties were left taking a "me too" position, or trying to divert the focus of the campaign to other issues. Neither of these strategies seemed to be succeeding and it looked as if REFORM could elect a majority of the city council, if it could just increase its support in the blue collar districts.

Funding. For the first time in its history REFORM had an adequate campaign chest. Individual donations had been easy to raise for this issue. Businesses had been generous, because they saw this solution to the solid waste problem as a means of keeping a cap on their taxes over the longer term. Also, the establishment of recycling facilities at municipal expense could reduce some of their own waste disposal costs.

Outside Help. A national coalition, Organizations United for Recycling (OUR), saw Fairfield as a test case and contributed funds. More important, it also contributed in-kind, by hiring an advertising agency to develop copy and ads that would be made available, at no cost, to any group or party that advocated OUR's cause. These materials "just happened" to fit precisely into REFORM's campaign in Fairfield. Since it was free and available to anyone who would use it, this in kind assistance did not show up in the campaign fund accounts as a large scale outside interference in Fairfield's affairs.

Media Budgeting

Because of its original populist thrust, engaging an advertising agency was unacceptable to the "powers that be" within REFORM. Dew Gueder, Consolidated Valve's Vice President of Marketing, had managed the advertising budget ever since REFORM had run its first candidate. In the past this had been no great task; there wasn't much to budget. They had spent the obligatory amount (see below) in the *Fairfield Star*, the daily newspaper, and then used whatever was left to have as many posters and lawn signs printed as possible. Funds for printing were divided evenly among the candidates running.

Dew was faced with an embarrassment of riches. He had real money to spend and, having arrived at his position with Consolidated through the sales route, did not feel particularly well qualified for the task. Over lunch with the owner of Consolidated's advertising agency, he learned that six media were probably best suited to REFORM's campaign.

Fairfield Star: the major daily newspaper serving Fairfield and the surrounding counties. Its circulation showed no pronounced demographic pattern. It was the voice of a prominent local family who were active in management. The paper was staunchly neutral in municipal politics. However, the publisher believed that, if a major local advertiser saw fit not to advertise in the Star, it reflected negatively on the paper's importance. He was rumored to have stated that any party not placing substantial advertising in the Star would find that there were "degrees of neutrality." Dew thought that about $20,000 would qualify as substantial, though he did not rule out spending a larger amount in the Star.

322

The Daily News: an upstart newspaper printed in tabloid format and having a decidedly down-scale bias in its circulation. It had started as an "on the lawn" neighborhood weekly. It now operated as a citywide daily, with a large and growing paid circulation. Its news coverage was limited almost entirely to Fairfield and the state. Some quipped that World War III could happen and it would not make the Daily News. It carried popular features by local writers, devoted to high school sports, hunting and fishing, auto repairs, and best buys at the supermarket.

Hi Lights: a glitzy, upscale local magazine, founded in 1982 and devoted to covering entertainment and the arts, restaurants, participation sports, and travel. It is delivered free to households in selected neighborhoods, and is otherwise available by subscription and on news stands. It has proven a huge success. Not many in Fairfield live "the good life," but many aspire to do so. Research indicates that those receiving the magazine, by whatever route, tend to read it from cover to cover. *Hi Lights* delivers a quality circulation and charges for it.

WFF–TV: the local CBS affiliate station. Thirty second spots on the evening news and "Featuring Fairfield", a local magazine show, were available and seemed affordable.

WFUN–AM: the only 50,000 watt AM station in the region. The programming varied little from day to day, featuring call-in shows, music weighted towards country-rock fusion, and more sports than many cared to hear. It's drive-time shows on week days were given over to information programming in a magazine format, unless a major league sports broadcast was in progress.

WFUN had a virtual monopoly on the midnight to dawn period, the only competition being WDUL, a small FM station, that alternated its music between classical and easy listening. Dew felt WFUN–AM's "After Midnight" could deliver an extremely attractive audience for REFORM's campaign, and spots here were relatively cheap. However, data on the size and composition of the audience was sketchy. Buying this time was largely a matter of faith.

Direct Mail: the direct mail house that handled Consolidated Valve's work was located in Fairfield and would manage a campaign for REFORM for out-of-pocket costs. Envelope stuffing, label pasting and other chores could be accomplished by party volunteers. REFORM's costs would consist of printing, postage and purchasing mailing lists. High quality lists of union members, and those who had been identified as targets during union organizing efforts were available from the local Council of Trade Leaders. You can control the number of addresses targeted, up to 1,000,000, in a mailing by changing the "circulation" for direct mail.

Costs and coverage for the media under consideration are summarized in Table 21. The data for WFUN are the station manager's own best estimates for the "After Midnight" show that Dew considered reasonable. All other information is from independent sources.

Table 21 Media Characteristics

	Fairfield Star	Daily News	Hi Lights	WFF TV	WFUN AM	Direct Mail
Rated Circulation(000)	3,109	1,567	300	1,889	1,500	1,000
% of Circulation Exposed	50	70	85	60	50	90
% of Exposed in Target Market	30	70	40	40	70	80
CPM	8.00	10.00	15.00	8.50	7.00	300.00

Copy experts at OUR's ad agency believed that the materials REFORM had obtained from OUR, which appealed to the self interest of the audience, would be effective with an average frequency in the target market of four exposures. Dew proposed, and REFORM's board agreed, that the *objective* would be to reach 65% of the target audience, subject to obtaining four effective exposures. $170,000 was available. However, REFORM had other expenses and would like to accomplish the advertising as cost effectively as possible.

The target was defined as households within the city limits in which at least one adult was employed in an occupation classified as blue collar, clerical, technical or retail sales. REFORM is, thus, targeting 2,534,000 of Fairfield's 5,268,000 residents. Coverage outside of the city was worth nothing.

Reaching REFORM's traditional supporters with the recycling message would largely be a matter of preaching to the converted. In fact, many supported the recycling cause out of notions of public spirit and sacrificing for the greater good. They might react negatively to the self-interest appeal.

Assignment

Select Promotion then the Advertising Reach and Frequency options from *The MART's* menus. Develop a budget allocation that will achieve REFORM's frequency objective and a reach of 60% as cheaply as possible.

(Remember, you enter dollar amounts in thousands of dollars. $1,000,000 is entered as 1000.)

1.   Enter your solution and its results below.

SOLUTION		RESULTS		
Media Vehicle	Budget	Performance Measure	Target Market	Total Population
Fairfield Star		Total Exposures		
Daily News		Reach		
Hi Lights		Average Frequency		
WFF–TV		Actual CPM		
WFUN–AM		Average Effective Exposures		Apply to Target Market Only
Direct Mail		CPM — Effective		
		Impact Score		

2. Data for "After Midnight" were extremely *iffy*. What effect would it have on your decision, if the proportion of its listeners in the target market were half as large as supposed?

SOLUTION		RESULTS		
Media Vehicle	Budget	Performance Measure	Target Market	Total Population
Fairfield Star		Total Exposures		
Daily News		Reach		
Hi Lights		Average Frequency		
WFF–TV		Actual CPM		
WFUN–AM		Average Effective Exposures		Apply to Target Market Only
Direct Mail		CPM — Effective		
		Impact Score		

3. What if the *Star* were to introduce a City Edition with a circulation of 2,400,000, 60% of circulation exposed, a CPM of $9.00, and of whose subscribers 65% were members of your target market? (*Reload* REFORM data to initialize values, then enter values for the city edition.) You may have to exceed your budget to achieve your reach and frequency objectives.

SOLUTION		RESULTS		
Media Vehicle	Budget	Performance Measure	Target Market	Total Population
Fairfield Star		Total Exposures		
Daily News		Reach		
Hi Lights		Average Frequency		
WFF–TV		Actual CPM		
WFUN–AM		Average Effective Exposures		Apply to Target Market Only
Direct Mail		CPM — Effective		
		Impact Score		

4. How would your allocations change, if your objective was to expose 60% of the entire population of Fairfield delivering an average of five exposures? (This can be taken from the top right hand portion of the results screen.) If you include the *Star* use the City Edition.

SOLUTION		RESULTS		
Media Vehicle	Budget	Performance Measure	Target Market	Total Population
Fairfield Star		Total Exposures		
Daily News		Reach		
Hi Lights		Average Frequency		
WFF–TV		Actual CPM		
WFUN–AM		Average Effective Exposures		Apply to Target Market Only
Direct Mail		CPM — Effective		
		Impact Score		

62 The Emporium

The Emporium, originally Goldschmidt's Department Store, was located in Fairfield. From 1873 until the late 1940's, Goldschmidt's had operated a single store in the city's central shopping district, serving the general population.

As the movement to the suburbs became pronounced, it became evident that Goldschmidt's was going to have to follow the population, if it was to prosper and grow. The first of many suburban branches, later called satellite stores, was opened in July of 1951. The city prospered until the mid seventies and Goldschmidt's grew apace.

Despite its growing size, Fairfield remained pretty much of a "lunch bucket town," dominated by firms like Consolidated Valve, its suppliers and subcontractors. Goldschmidt's continued to pursue a policy of having something for everyone, with emphasis on lower priced lines having a mass appeal.

A New Strategy

Beginning around 1975, competition with the discount stores for the low end of the market became brutal. In 1986, Goldschmidt sought the help of Focus, a management consulting firm that had close ties to the Limited chain. Following a careful study of the trends in a newly diversifying Fairfield, the Focus report recommended a radical change in strategy. After much debate, soul searching and internal strife, the board of directors decided to adopt most of the Focus team's recommendations. Two vice presidents and several senior buyers resigned on the spot.

In the fall of 1987, the downtown flagship store and about half of the satellite stores were sold to an Indianapolis based retailer. The purchaser already owned a small chain of discount stores with which Goldschmidt's had competed. In early 1988, the remaining stores closed their doors. Inventory was disposed of at fire sale prices. Later in the year, The Emporium arose, Phoenix like, from the ashes of Goldschmidt's.

The remaining stores were all located in the upscale white collar suburbs, where all of Fairfield's net growth was taking place. The proceeds of the asset sale was used to redecorate and restock these stores, and to move several to more desirable, and more expensive space. Internally, each store was designed and managed as a collection of boutiques. All stores had the same set of boutiques. Individual store managers had considerable freedom in deciding how the space and budgets would be allocated among them.

329

Media Budgeting

Buying and advertising were centralized. Victoria Spring was the Emporium's Advertising Manager. In addition to her supervisory duties, she took on the task of allocating the media budget among the various alternatives herself.

Determining media budgets had been a simple matter at Goldschmidt's. With its mass circulation, the *Fairfield Star* was well suited to the store's needs. Other than some token spending in a variety of news letters and house organs, budgeting was a matter of negotiating rates and schedules with the Star's sales manager. Goldschmidt's was an important enough account, for the newspaper's business manager, and even the publisher to take an interest.

An Experiment

The Emporium, from its birth, had utilized a wider range of print media. Last year during the Christmas season, they had successfully experimented with television and decided to continue to use it.

The Spring Campaign

Given the success of their first use of a nonprint medium, Victoria had decided to venture further afield. In addition to ads for newspaper, magazine and television, she had her staff develop copy for radio ads, featuring the Emporium's Teen Town youth boutiques.

Objectives

The objectives for the season's advertising were to reach 60% of the members of households with annual incomes above the median with an average of four effective exposures. These individuals were estimated to account for 1,644,000 of Fairfield's 5,268,000 residents.

Media Under Consideration

Victoria was willing to consider any of Fairfield's publishers and broadcasters, if it accomplished her objective. (See Media descriptions in the REFORM case.) If she used WFF-TV she would purchase prime time spots. The evening drive time show on WFUN-AM was under consideration. It featured a dress-for-success type feature twice a week. Since radio was somewhat experimental, Victoria had decided to limit her total spending on this medium to no more than one fifth of her budget ($50,000).

Brochures promoting merchandise and sales events were regularly piggybacked with monthly bills. Corporate policy ruled out other uses of direct mail.

WROK–FM was under consideration for the Teen Town spots. The station alternated on an hourly basis between current hits and golden oldies from the sixties and seventies.

Campaign Theme

In planning for the Spring and Easter season, "Affordable Fashion for the Discerning Family," had been selected as the concept to be stressed in Emporium advertising. Any radio executions of the season's campaign will involve image advertising for the store, rather than attempting to promote specific merchandise.

Costs and coverage for the media under consideration are summarized in Table 22. All information is from independent sources.

Table 22 Media Characteristics

	Fairfield Star	Daily News	Hi Lights	WFF TV	WFUN AM	WROK FM
Rated Circulation (000)	3109	1567	300	1889	1500	952
% of Circulation Exposed	50	70	80	60	50	70
% of Exposed in Target Market	20	10	75	20	50	80
CPM	8.00	10.00	15.00	8.50	7.00	12.00

Assignment

Select Promotion and then the Reach and Frequency option from *The MART's* menus. Develop a budget allocation that will achieve The Emporium's advertising objectives. Victoria's budget is $250,000. Higher level management views the reach and frequency objectives as conservative. If it came to a choice, they would rather achieve greater reach, subject to maintaining an average of four effective exposure, than have the budget underspent.

(Remember, you enter dollar amounts in thousands of dollars. $1,000,000 is entered as 1000.)

1. Enter your solution and its results below.

SOLUTION		RESULTS		
Media Vehicle	Budget	Performance Measure	Target Market	Total Population
Fairfield Star		Total Exposures		
Daily News		Reach		
Hi Lights		Average Frequency		
WFF–TV		Actual CPM		
WFUN–AM		Average Effective Exposures		Apply to Target Market Only
WROK – FM		CPM — Effective		
		Impact Score		

2. What effect would it have on your solution, if only 30% of *Hi Lights* exposures were in your target market?

SOLUTION		RESULTS		
Media Vehicle	Budget	Performance Measure	Target Market	Total Population
Fairfield Star		Total Exposures		
Daily News		Reach		
Hi Lights		Average Frequency		
WFF–TV		Actual CPM		
WFUN– AM		Average Effective Exposures		Apply to Target Market Only
WROK — FM		CPM — Effective		
		Impact Score		

3. What if the *Daily News* were to introduce a Suburban Edition with a circulation of 500,000, 70% of circulation exposed, a CPM of $12.00, and 60% of whose subscribers were members of your target market? (*Reload* Emporium data to initialize values, then enter values for the Suburban Edition.)

SOLUTION		RESULTS		
Media Vehicle	Budget	Performance Measure	Target Market	Total Population
Fairfield Star		Total Exposures		
Daily News		Reach		
Hi Lights		Average Frequency		
WFF–TV		Actual CPM		
WFUN–AM		Average Effective Exposures		Apply to Target Market Only
WROK – FM		CPM — Effective		
		Impact Score		

4. How would your allocations change, if your objective was to reach 60% of the entire population of Fairfield, delivering an average of five exposures? If you use the *Daily News*, use the Suburban Edition. (This can be taken from the top right hand portion of the results screen.)

SOLUTION		RESULTS		
Media Vehicle	Budget	Performance Measure	Target Market	Total Population
Fairfield Star		Total Exposures		
Daily News		Reach		
Hi Lights		Average Frequency		
WFF–TV		Actual CPM		
WFUN– AM		Average Effective Exposures		Apply to Target Market Only
WROK – FM		CPM — Effective		
		Impact Score		